Gardener's Companion Series

The Virginia Gardener's Companion

An Insider's Guide to Low-Maintenance Gardening in Virginia

Donna Williamson

Guilford, Connecticut

Copyright © 2008 by Morris Book Publishing, LLC

Text design by Casey Shain
Illustrations by Josh Yunger
Map by M. A. Dubé © Morris Book Publishing, LLC

Library of Congress Cataloging-in-Publication Data

Williamson, Donna.
  The Virginia gardener's companion : an insiders guide to
low-maintenance gardening in Virginia / Donna Williamson.
    p. cm. — (Gardener's companion series)
  Includes index.
  ISBN-13: 978-0-7627-4311-7
  1. Gardening—Virginia. I. Title. II. Series.
  SB451.34.V8W55 2008
  635.09755—dc22

                                                                2008003836

Printed in the United States of America

10 9 8 7 6 5 4 3 2 1

To all the gardeners who have shared so much

Contents

Introduction

Many Virginia gardeners look longingly at garden books showing beautiful settings of daylilies blooming alongside daisies, irises, roses, and phlox. If you're like me and have tried to replicate those picture-perfect plant combinations, you've discovered that those combos may thrive in Massachusetts, but they don't bloom together that way in Virginia. Instead, the Virginia gardener needs to choose different plant combinations for our long growing season—those combinations that don't rely on crisp New England weather and that are happy in local conditions.

The Virginia Gardener's Companion is designed to help you make the most of your gardening experience. It explains how you can develop good plant combinations and garden in a relaxed, easy, low-maintenance way.

The low-maintenance approach suits most gardeners today, especially as so many demands on our time might otherwise crowd gardening from our lives. I have gardened the hard way, and I know firsthand that the low-maintenance way is better. Apply newspaper sheets topped with compost or chopped leaves to get rid of grass in an expanded garden area. Use ground covers or perennials as ground covers to eliminate the need for mulch. Plant drifts of ornamental grasses over spring bulbs. Apply shredded leaves and compost to the garden to feed most trees and shrubs—no need to buy and apply fertilizers. These are just a few of the proven techniques I've learned from experience and other gardeners. You'll find some of my favorite techniques in sidebars titled "Donna's Best Advice."

Gardening can be a satisfying, fascinating, and lifelong pastime when you have good basic information. To that end, I work to dispel gardening myths and counter commonly dispensed but out-of-date information that confuses gardeners. In short, this book cuts through the nonsense and presents information that works with Virginia's soil and climate. My goal is to help you stay close to nature and the basic principles of gardening so that you can make good choices, have success, and find joy in your time in the garden.

Being in the garden is for good days and bad. On September 11, 2001, I was preparing to travel to a conference at Norfolk Botanical Garden. Late in the afternoon, a conference organizer called me and said, "Some of the speakers can't get here but we are going ahead with the conference. We think being in the garden will help." It did. It restored and reconnected me with the natural world.

Becoming a gardener brings you gifts. Opportunities to observe the power and detail of nature, the cycle and variation of the seasons, the resilience and endurance of trees, and even the changes in the sky are fresh, constant, and free. They give you perspective and calm. Eating a tomato you grew from seed and watching a tree you planted get tall and strong are delights that resonate. Knowledge, experience, and confidence increase over the years, and gardens and gardeners relax.

Whatever comes, being in the garden helps.

There are many people involved in writing a book. Some are dear friends who wrestle the finer points with you; some are masters of detailed information that round out a subject. My gratitude is deep and wide to these talented and generous people: Art Stern, Debbie Dillion, Cole Burrell, Michael Mendias, Peter Loewer, Dr. Lee Daniels, Martha Slover, Pat Reilly, Joan Butler, Mary Danewitz, Grace and Charlie Wakefield, Paula Brisco, Mary Foran, Genie Cate, Connie Nash, Lauren Springer, Jane Duane, Linda Chalker-Scott, Leo Schweiger, Rick Darke, Barb Gibson, Pam Harper, Ed Milhous, Sydney Eddison, Peter Deahl, Ammie and Jerry Conner, Shawn Askew, Lou Verner, Carol Heiser, Mike Goatley, Mac Stiff, David Roos, Peg Riccio, Liz Borst, Ginny Spoon, Nancy and Zane Carter, Brent Heath, Frank Johnson, Rita Buchanan, Ben Tennyson, Bonnie Appleton, Karen Rexrode, Pat Wing, Linda and Dean Linderman, Kathy Gibb, and Marilyn Janaczek. You made this possible. Many thanks.

Firm
Foundations

Soil Basics

It is easier to work with nature than to be in a constant struggle with the seasons, the climate, the soils, and other factors. Choosing the right kinds of gardens for your site and lifestyle and working in concert with nature will give you a delightful, low-maintenance landscape to enjoy. Let's start by gaining insight into the factors that can affect your garden plans and design choices.

The Elements of Soil: Clay, Silt, and Sand

When one looks at Virginia today, it is hard to believe that hundreds of millions of years ago our state had Himalayan-type mountains. In the intervening millennia, Virginia's mountains have eroded, fallen, slid, and been windblown bit by bit, each rock fragmenting into smaller and smaller particles across the breadth of the state. These rock particles make up the bulk of what we call soil.

Soil is made of inorganic and organic material.

Inorganic material. As rocks and minerals weather, they break into smaller inorganic particles. These particles resist change, so that a granite rock will keep its chemical composition no matter what size it becomes.

From biggest to smallest, soil particles run from coarse gravel to fine gravel, coarse sand, fine sand, sandy loam, loam, silt loam, silt, and finally clay. Coarse gravel is about 4 millimeters in size. Silt is about 0.5 to 0.002 millimeter. A clay particle is smaller than 0.002 millimeter.

Sand particles are loose and don't hold together. They cannot bind to minerals, hold on to nutrients, or retain water. Yet soils with a lot of sand are rich in oxygen, warm up quickly in spring, and drain quickly. Sandy soils can be worked even when wet, and they are good for early flowers; for bulbs, tubers, and root vegetables; and for heat-loving vegetables like cantaloupe, tomatoes, and pumpkins.

Silt particles cannot bind minerals either, but water attaches a bit better to silt than to sand yet not as well as to clay.

Microscopic clay particles have a negative charge, which attracts water molecules. As a result, clay soils retain water and are often fertile, holding minerals and nutrients as well. Some soils with a lot of clay don't have enough space for air to circulate so they drain poorly and become waterlogged, forming a sticky soil. Clay soils warm slowly in spring and cannot be worked when wet. They are best suited for late-maturing plants.

Organic material. The other part of soil is organic: humus (that is, decomposed plants), living insects, bacteria, fungi, algae, worms, insect debris, leaves, soil creatures undergoing decomposition, and plants. The organic components help to build soil structure while making mineral nutrients available in forms

Evaluate Your Soil

You can conduct your own soil experiment. Use an empty glass jar, perhaps a mayonnaise jar, and scoop a few cups of your garden soil into it. Add one or two drops of dish soap to ease mixing and fill the jar with tap water. Close the lid and shake well. You will see a cloud of muddy water. Let the soil test jar sit for a day. Soil particles will separate into bands by size and weight, enabling you to roughly judge soil composition. The sand particles will be on the bottom, the silt layer in the middle, and the clay layer with organic material on top.

plants can take up. Organic matter increases both soil permeability and water-holding capacity. It takes a lot of organic material, about 20 percent of the entire soil volume, to make an organically rich soil. Since organic matter is always undergoing the decomposition process, new organic material needs to be added annually.

Soils in Virginia

All in all, Virginia has more than 750 distinctive soil types, according to soil scientist Professor W. Lee Daniels of Virginia Polytechnic Institute and State University (Virginia Tech). In any given county there are thirty to forty distinctive soils! The differences are due primarily to the underlying rock or sediment type and the soil's landscape position—on top of a hill, on a slope, or in a drainway.

In most valleys of Virginia, the soils are deep and old. The Shenandoah Valley contains the remnants of a seabed formed by reef-building algae, and the resulting limestone is high in calcium and magnesium but low in other minerals necessary for good plant growth.

The western mountain areas feature limestone caverns and coal. Soils in this region range from deep, clay soils to shallow, rocky soils. East of the Blue Ridge, tiny pockets of serpentine rock and soil are remnants of earlier tectonic collisions. In these areas and a few other parts of Virginia, the soil's mineral composition can be unusual and needs amendment to offset very acid pockets of soil or high levels of metals like zinc. Your local Cooperative Extension staff can help identify these specific, unusual areas.

Between the Blue Ridge and the fall line, the elevation drops, and the Piedmont stretches across half of Virginia. Here we find variable clay soils atop a mix of igneous and metamorphic rocks. In the longer growing season of the sandier southern Piedmont, where tobacco was once king, farmers now cultivate peanuts, cotton, and other crops.

Coastal Plain soils benefit from nutrient-rich alluvial deposits brought by river flooding, but these soils contain significant proportions of sand. Plants growing there can suffer badly in drought conditions. East of Interstate 95, the soils of the Coastal Plain become even sandier. On the Eastern Shore the soils are prone to constant loss of nutrients as water leaches nutrients through the sand.

Facing Your Virginia Soil Challenges

While the old expression "don't fight the site" really means you can't easily change the soil on your property, you *can* improve the soil in the areas where you garden. Let's look at some of Virginia's challenging soils and examine effective techniques by soil type.

Clay soils. The most common clay of Virginia is considered "low in charge, an ability to retain macro- and micronutrients," according to W. Lee Daniels. Most locations have a layer of topsoil over clay. But when clay soil is exposed at the surface (common in new home sites where topsoil is stripped), the clay soil can be dense and sticky (if moist) or hard (if dry). It is made workable with compost or other organic materials that improve its texture and porosity. Fortunately, clay particles have good water-holding properties that benefit gardeners in the summer drought cycle. With several exceptions—brickyards and locations where the clay has a propensity to shrink and swell badly—it is good to have a moderate amount of clay (10 to 20 percent) in your soil.

What if you have too much clay? Adding sand to a clayey soil will not counterbalance clay's tough, plastic nature unless you add very large amounts of sand, about 50 percent of the soil's volume. You could remove half of your soil, replace it with sand, and then till the whole volume together to a depth of about 2 feet— but that would be a massive undertaking. Another approach, amending only the planting hole, is a recipe for failure, because what that does is create a bowl where the plant will drown when water fails to drain out.

What then can you do to improve clay soil? The answer is to

apply composted organic material. Composts help to lighten and loosen heavy clay soils over time as humus accumulates and the soil particles aggregate and develop good structure. Adding organic material is practical, economical, and effective.

Sandy soils on the Coastal Plain and Eastern Shore are typically low in potassium because that water-soluble mineral goes where the water goes—right through the coarse sand particles in soils. Adding compost and organic amendments to sand will retain water, slow leaching, and retain potassium and other valuable nutrients.

Wetlands. The Coastal Plain and the bay side of the Eastern Shore include large wetlands where acid-loving trees and ericaceous plants thrive. Matthews County, for instance, is 50 to 60 percent wetlands. Silty and organically rich soils often appear in these areas. There is no need to improve soil in these areas. Rather, consider using a palette of moisture-loving plants to increase interest and diversity in wetland gardens.

Shale and stone. The most difficult natural areas for gardeners are hilly areas where shale conditions predominate. All the major ridges are capped with sandstone and generally hold very little plant-available water. In addition, the existing soils are in shallow layers over broken rock, and water runs off the hills rather than penetrates the soil. According to Daniels, the two best approaches for gardeners in those areas are to grow plants in raised beds and berms or to stick to native plants that can tolerate dry, acidic, rocky situations. (More about these two strategies later.)

Shenandoah Valley soils. Soils in the Shenandoah Valley are deep, except for areas of rock outcrops. These valley soils are quite old, and their natural fertility is low. They can be made very productive with the addition of organic matter and fertilizers to balance minerals.

River floodplain and valley soils. Famous "Pamunkey" soils exist along the former floodplains of the James and other Virginia rivers. Considered "beautiful" by both soil scientists and

The New-Home Subsoil Blues

Soil problems resulting from the complete removal of topsoil by builders are common and difficult for the homeowner. Subsoil can be sticky and dense when all the humus-rich top-soil has been removed (and sold) and when the soil has been compacted and all its air squeezed out by earth-moving equipment and vehicle traffic. It's no fun to plant in this type of soil. The remedy? Add lots of compost. While it takes some time and has some limitations, applying organic mate-rial with additional nutrients and minerals (depending on the results of your soil test) is an effective approach. Another option is to build a berm, an easy way to form new planting beds that can resolve most soil problems. More on soil tests and berms later.

gardeners, these deep, nutrient-rich soils make for easy gardening and are among the most productive in Virginia. Soil compaction can be a problem with alluvial soils, so install and keep to walk-ways. Avoid the urge to overfertilize; keep the soils "beautiful" by adding organic material each year.

pH 101

Another common gardening feature in Virginia is acidic soil. Ninety percent of the soils of Virginia have an acid pH, even in the Shenandoah Valley, where the underlying parent rock is lime-stone. Acidic soils are typical of the rainy and humid East Coast. Once you know the pH of your soil, you can choose plants that thrive in those conditions.

The term pH means potential hydrogen. It is a measurement of how alkaline or acidic the soil is. The pH scale runs from 0 to 14. The midpoint of 7 is considered neutral—neither acid nor alkaline. As pH numbers decrease, acidity increases. Numbers above 7 signify increases in alkalinity. Very low (below 4) or very high (above 8.5) numbers mean the soil generally will not support normal plant life.

The pH scale is logarithmic. The difference between two numbers is not a unit of one but a multiple of ten. For instance, a pH of 5 is ten times more acid than a pH of 6. You can see why it would be hard to change pH. Your soil volume is huge and would require equally huge amounts of acidifying or alkalizing agents to move the pH even a small amount. Beyond that, it would not be a permanent change; over time the pH would revert because the parent material has not changed. It's best to play to your strengths and find great plants that suit your soil.

How does pH affect plant growth? Very acid (or, in contrast, very alkaline) soils can bind up essential nutrients in odd ways. Some plants are unable to access needed nutrients when soils are too acid or too alkaline. Alkaline areas can make iron, manganese, copper, zinc, and boron unavailable to plants. Calcium and molybdenum can become unavailable in very acidic soils. Phosphorus can become unavailable if either extreme is found.

Most plants like a pH of 5.5 to 7.0. Blueberries, dogwoods, camellias, hollies, magnolias, rhododendrons, and heathers like very acid soil, around a pH of 4.5. Other plants—like asparagus, beets, lilacs, and lawn grasses—prefer alkaline soil.

Most plants grow very well in Virginia's acidic soils. When your soils are at the extreme ends of the "happy range," you may need to make adjustments. I have very acid soils (pH range 4.5 to 5.0), and yet I grow roses, magnolias, dogwoods, and many other beauties. The only area that gets lime is the asparagus bed.

Lime is an alkaline salt of calcium. Dolomitic lime is a good form for gardeners to use because it also contains magnesium. According to Debbie Dillion, Loudoun County's urban horticulturist, if you need to lime existing areas to make them less acidic, top-dress with no more than fifty pounds per 1,000 square feet per application. That's as much lime as the soil can handle at one

Lime and Lawns

People routinely spread limestone on their lawns so the grass in acid soils will be healthier. One word of caution: You can spread too much lime on the lawn, resulting in highly alkaline soil. If the pH is too high, minerals get tied up and are unavailable to plants. Lawn grasses like a pH between 6.2 and 6.8. Above that, the plants will be weakened and more susceptible to diseases that can damage them. A soil test will tell you if you need lime at all and will provide advice on how much you need.

time. You sprinkle the lime on top of the soil so that it trickles down with rain. Spring and fall applications seem to suit most people, as those seasons usually have reliable rainfall.

You are not likely to have acid pH issues with plantings next to concrete foundations or walkways. Concrete leaches lime and can make the soil less acidic. Often plants chosen for placement at foundations and walkways are favorites like holly or rhododendrons (including azaleas), but these plants require highly acidic soil. Place them alongside concrete and they struggle and look tatty. Instead, consider using plants that tolerate the higher pH near concrete, such as boxwood, Saint-John's-wort, redbud, and clematis.

Start with a Soil Test

No matter what your soil challenges, there are ways to make your situation better.

The folks at the Cooperative Extension offices across the state recommend a soil test as your first step to a better garden. Test soil from each area of your landscape that you wish to plant in. This will help identify and correct any unbalanced mineral components.

Virginia Tech and several private labs provide soil-testing services that give you a report on your soil's pH, its levels of major mineral components, and suggested amounts and types of amendments to improve your soil.

For instance, Virginia Tech's local Cooperative Extension offices provide test kits that include a small cardboard box to contain your soil sample and a "Soil Sample Information Sheet for Home Lawns, Gardens, Fruits, and Ornamentals" for you to complete.

Use one soil-test box for each separate area you plan to develop into a garden. Using a trowel or shovel, take several samples in a zigzag pattern, digging about 6 to 10 inches deep. If soils change visibly in a section of your garden, a separate sample should be taken. Don't dig wet soils. Place the samples in a clean pail; remove grass, plants, stones, and sticks. Mix the soil together in the pail and then fill the cardboard box. Put an identifier on the box, like "veg-grdn."

When you submit the sample, tell the testing folks what you plan to grow: roses, grapes, trees, vegetables, whatever. The routine test for pH, phosphorus, potassium, and minor nutrients is $7 per sample. Send samples in a sturdy carton with your payment to Virginia Tech Soil Testing Lab, 145 Smyth Hall (0465), Blacksburg, VA 24061.

Private soil-testing labs are also available in Virginia. Some people use A & L Eastern Laboratories, Inc. in Richmond (804-743-9401; www.al-labs-eastern.com), which offers results via e-mail.

Once you have your soil test results and recommendations, what's next? In most areas of Virginia, all that gardeners need do to improve their soil is to add (and continue to add!) composted

Donna's Best Advice: Berms

After nearly two decades of garden design, installation, and maintenance, I have figured some things out when it comes to improving soil and gardening in a low-maintenance way. Take the British concept of double-digging. I could never embrace the idea of moving clay lumps from one hole to another. Then there's the common practice of tilling. For years I blended nutritious amendments like colloidal rock phosphate, greensand, manure, and kelp into the soil. Unfortunately, every time I tilled I brought up every weed seed deposited in the last millennium and gave each seed an opportunity to germinate and grow lushly in the well-fertilized plot. The result was a glorious bed of weeds among the perennials.

Things are different now. There is no more tilling with its resulting destruction of the soil structure and the creatures that make the soil a living organism. Weeds are minimal. How do I do it? My secret: berms. Here's how I build them.

I cover the grass with five sheets of newspaper (no plastic) and then add loads of chopped leaves, manure, some sand, leaf compost, and finely chopped pine bark to a depth of 2 to 3 feet. Then I plant into the berm. Areas that are not immediately planted benefit from a 1- to 2-inch layer of mulch made of finely chopped pine bark, straw over newspaper, or chopped leaves. As with any new garden bed, you will need to water plants regularly until they are well established. But you'll find that plants get a fast start in the berm, and over time they extend their roots down through the decomposing newspaper and dead grass litter and into the underlying native soil.

The berm shrinks as the organic material decomposes and settles down into native soil. So each year I apply a fresh layer of organic material.

Berms. No weed explosion, no heavy digging, and all the joys of gardening without the pain.

organic materials—household compost, horse manure, leaf compost, leafy weeds, spoiled straw, dead fish, seaweed, grass clippings, etc. Organic material loosens clay and fills in the gaps of sandy soils. It percolates down into subsoil and feeds soil bacteria, beneficial nematodes, earthworms, and other soil dwellers. These creatures help aggregate soil particles, improving the structure and the drainage characteristics of the soil. Organic matter builds the next layer of topsoil.

Food for Soil

Adding organic materials to the soil is the most beneficial and least costly way to improve the soil's structure, moisture-holding ability, and drainage and to increase populations of healthy soil flora and fauna. The flora and fauna are important because they act on soil components like minerals, manure, and humus and make them available in solution to feed plants. Keep in mind that plants take up nutrients in liquid form.

The following organic components will improve your soil no matter what you decide to grow.

Compost is decomposed material and can be made from stuff like kitchen waste, leafy weeds (but not their seeds), cow pies, and dog hair. Composts are made of "green" and "brown" materials. Green ingredients include apple peels, grass clippings, outer lettuce leaves, and overcooked pasta. Brown ingredients include old cornstalks, straw (not hay), and dried grass. You can alternate layers of green and brown ingredients. From time to time apply a shovelful of native soil over the green layer; this brings minerals, clay particles, and microorganisms to the compost. According to Eliot Coleman, organic gardening guru and author of *The New Organic Grower*, straw is the engine driving the composting process. Its hollow stems allow good aeration, and the carbon to nitrogen ratio is high, encouraging the decomposition process.

Alfalfa meal is a source of nitrogen and potassium (about 2 percent each) as well as growth stimulants for the garden. It is a green component for the compost pile.

Autumn leaves can be put in a bin created by snow fencing or pallets and allowed to decompose on their own. Chopping the leaves speeds the decomposition process that is caused by fungi. Eventually the leaves become leaf mold, an excellent addition to any garden soil.

Manures have been used for centuries, but please don't add fresh manure to the garden! Nitrogen compounds (ammonia) in fresh manure can volatilize rapidly, burning nearby plants. Well-rotted and decomposed manure is safe to use as a side-dressing around plants or added to the compost pile. While most composted manures are not very high in nutrients, they provide good organic material and improve the soil's water-holding capacity and texture. Manure plus water equals manure tea, and since manure tea is already in solution, it adds nutrients quickly to plants.

Fertilizers can be quick or slow acting. Those that act quickly feed the plant and not the soil. In contrast, slow- and long-acting minerals can help build improved soil over a period of years.

Plant Nutrients: The ABCs of NPK

Most packages of fertilizers have numbers on them, like 10-10-10 or 0-0-4.5. These numbers relate to the percentage of nitrogen (N), phosphorus (P), and potassium (K), by weight, in the fertilizer. All plants need these three macronutrients in balanced amounts.

Nitrogen is needed during the growing season for good green leaf and stem growth. It is used up quickly, volatilizes into the air, and leaches out of the soil with water, so it is important to add nitrogen each spring to give plants a good start. If plants are pale and spindly, a light feeding of nitrogen may solve the problem.

Nitrogen should to be added each year for vegetable and annual plantings. Manure, alfalfa, dead fish, kelp, or other nitrogen-rich materials are all good. Watch out for amendments like cottonseed meal—it's high in nitrogen, but cottonseed is a heavily treated crop, and cottonseed meal may contain pesticide residue.

Too much nitrogen can be detrimental to plants, causing excessive leafy growth and attracting insects and disease. Usually, the life and death of animals, insects, and soil creatures that occur in the surrounding soil provide adequate amounts of nitrogen for perennial and woody plants and trees, and no additional supplementation is necessary.

Phosphorus is an important element for disease resistance and root development. It is crucial to the development of fruit and seeds. Colloidal (soft) rock phosphate contains about 16 percent phosphorus and 19 percent calcium and is more quickly available for plants to take up than hard rock phosphate. One application will last for several years. Apply at the rate of about ten pounds per 100 square feet. You may need something quick-acting for annuals and vegetables, such as the highly soluble superphosphate and triple superphosphate. But be warned that you can go overboard here and create a mineral imbalance. Top-dress lightly and let the fertilizer seep into the soil. Or, if you are tilling, add about one-quarter pound of superphosphate per square yard of soil about 1 foot deep.

Potassium is important for growth and disease resistance. Greensand is a slow-acting form of potassium combined with micronutrients. This form is not highly soluble and must be worked on by soil creatures before the potassium can be taken up by plants. It is a long-term soil builder. Quick acting muriate of potash will make soluble potassium available to quick turnaround plants like annuals and vegetables; follow the label directions.

Micronutrients

Plants need trace amounts of many minerals for good health. Boron, calcium, chlorine, copper, iron, magnesium, manganese, molybdenum, sulfur, and zinc are necessary in teeny amounts. Most soils already contain these micronutrients. Unless the pH is unusual or there is an overabundance of some mineral, application of micronutrients is usually unnecessary. However, plants grown in containers with soilless mixes will need complete fertilizers that include trace elements.

Other Soil Amendments

You may have heard of some of the following products that may improve your soil and gardening ease:

Alfalfa, a nitrogen-fixing plant, is a gentle source of nitrogen when sprinkled in the garden. It also has a growth hormone on board. I use alfalfa meal, available from feed stores, blended into piles of wood chips or mulch to help quicken the decomposition process. I also apply alfalfa meal around roses.

Blood meal is powdered blood from slaughtered animals. It is high in nitrogen (14 percent) and is reputed to repel deer and rabbits. It attracts dogs, skunks, and carrion eaters.

Bonemeal can also attract animals, including rats, but it contains about 11 percent phosphorus and 22 percent calcium. It's good for bulbs and tomatoes.

Corn gluten meal is a by-product of corn processing and contains about 10 percent nitrogen. If used early in the growing season, it acts as a mild herbicide by interfering with the development of seedlings. So don't use corn gluten if you are growing plants from seed. It is safe to use with actively growing plants.

Epsom salts contain magnesium (10 percent) and sulfur (13 percent). Epsom salts are reputed to strengthen cell walls. Roses and tomatoes "seem" to benefit from a tablespoon around the base of the plant, but this is an old-time gardener's practice and may be wishful thinking. It lacks scientific proof.

Fish by-products are great fertilizers. Liquid forms can be mixed with water and used every couple of weeks. The smell, even when "deodorized," is often useful in repelling deer. Fish meal (or dead fish parts) can be used for sheet composting, in which the gardener digs a hole near actively growing plants, drops the fish into the hole, and covers it with soil.

Greensand is mined in the ocean off the New Jersey coast and contains potassium (3 percent) and micronutrients. Soil creatures convert it to plant-available potassium. The conversion occurs slowly over time as microorganisms work on the greensand. This

Rethinking Hydrogels

"Water crystals" sold at nurseries to ease watering responsibilities actually lock up available water and prevent plants from accessing it, according to research conducted by Dr. Bonnie Appleton of Virginia Tech's Hampton Roads Agricultural Research and Extension Center. It's like trying to get a drink of water from Jell-O. In addition, some of these polyacrylamide hydrogels (polymers of acrylamide and potassium acrylate) are composed of toxic compounds that decompose into depolymerized water-soluble acrylamide units that may be short-lived but are carcinogenic and lethal neurotoxins. In less acid soils, this process can take up to two years. In Virginia's acid soils, decomposition is much quicker. Additionally, hydrogels don't work well in clay. These substances are especially dangerous in waterways and can kill fish and other aquatic creatures. We are lucky, I guess, because Virginia's acidic soil decomposes the crystals so rapidly that their use is even more questionable. New research is under way to develop starch-based gels for garden and landscape use as alternatives. Cultural practices of adding organic materials, leaves, and composts to soils to retain moisture are more effective, less costly, and harmless by comparison.

Consult the thoughtful work of Dr. Linda Chalker-Scott on this and other topics at www.puyallup.wsu.edu/%7Linda%20 Chalker-Scott/index.html.

slow process builds potassium reserves in the soil over years.

Kelp/seaweed meal can add valuable micronutrients. You can make seaweed tea for a quick plant boost.

Limestone reduces acidity in soils and, according to Lee Daniels of Virginia Tech, helps in aggregating soil particles and improving soil structure. The components of different forms of limestone are variable. I prefer dolomitic lime, which is roughly 46 percent calcium and 38 percent magnesium.

Nitrate of soda is a fast-acting granular form of nitrogen (about 16 percent) mined in Chile. It contains salt, so use it sparingly.

Soybean meal is available in pellet form and has about 7 percent nitrogen.

Whatever you choose to use to improve your garden's soil, keep in mind that a plan for feeding the *soil* over time is a winning strategy, with better long-term results than feeding today's *plant*.

When to Fertilize

Your soil test will indicate if there is an imbalance in nutrients in your soil. You will get information about the types and amounts of amendments to add for good growth of the plants you identified as wanting to grow. Continue to add leaf mold and other organics, like compost, each year. If your soil is naturally well balanced, additional light application of fertilizer is needed only for certain high-nutrient-demanding fruit trees, vegetables, and annuals.

Different types of plants have varying nutrient needs.

Shrubs and trees. In general, well-planted woody plants and trees in good soil grow well without fertilizers. Lack of fertilization is rarely the cause of tree problems, despite all the advertising to the contrary.

Perennials. Most perennials are not demanding and find adequate nutrition in decent soils. For roses, a top-dressing of manure or alfalfa applied in the spring and during the breathing spells is beneficial. Excessive stimulation of plants, especially with nitrogen, will produce big, leafy growth that attracts insect predators and interferes with the plants' ability to harden off for winter.

Vegetables and annuals. Plants with just one season to do all their growing, like most vegetables and annuals, benefit from fertilization. Tomatoes, zinnias, and pumpkins will be happy with a balanced approach. Not too much nitrogen, please, or you will have fat leaves and poor flowering and fruiting.

Time-release fertilizers are easy to use. They slowly dissolve and leak a bit of fertilizer each time rains fall or you water. They are convenient but they run out of fertilizer well before summer ends. Reapply in mid-July. Fertilizers added to water are fast acting because they are already in solution. For annuals, vegetables, and container plants, I use half-strength liquid fertilizer every two weeks in addition to the slow-release spheres mixed in the soil.

Fertilization should only occur *after the plant is well watered*. A drought-stressed plant can be mortally affected by a swift shot of fertilizer.

A plant that is not doing well is unlikely to be helped by a big shot of fertilizer. Poor plant choice for conditions, poor drainage, improper planting techniques, critter or string-trimmer damage, inadequate water, and inhospitable soil conditions are critical factors. Fertilizer won't fix those problems. Taking the time to feed the soil with composts, manures, and essential minerals will serve your garden far better in the long term rather than just feeding a certain set of plants.

Your Site

One of the keys to success in the garden is planting trees, shrubs, perennials, grasses, bulbs, and ground covers that will thrive in your specific climate and landscape situation.

Climate in Virginia is influenced by our latitude, which ranges from 36° to 39° north of the equator. Generally mild winters and long, hot summers give us a moderate climate, and we have a bounty of plants to choose from. There are some plants that are not long lived in Virginia because of the heat—white birch, poplar, delphinium, and lupine, for example—but we are a horticultural fringe where many northern and southern plants thrive.

Naturally, elevation and physical features like mountains and bodies of water affect our climate. In the eastern part of the state, Chesapeake Bay and the Atlantic Ocean moderate temperatures in winter and reduce the likelihood of late spring freezes. At the higher elevations of the western ridge and valley areas, late freezes and frosts are common. Most storms move parallel to the Appalachian and Blue Ridge Mountains, in a northeasterly direction. Coastal storms can bring occasional heavy rainfall or snow to the mountain and Piedmont areas, but heavy snow is rare in the southern Piedmont, Coastal Plain, and Eastern Shore.

In the Zone

Zone maps can be useful guides as you begin to build your garden. They tell you approximately how cold typical winters will be and how hot to expect the summer.

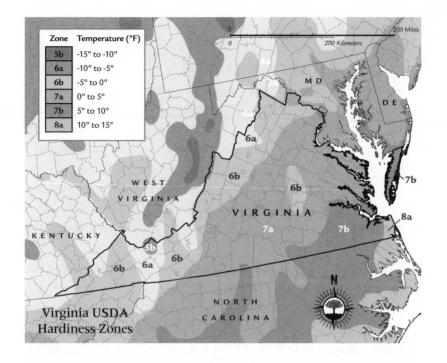

Zone	Temperature (°F)
5b	-15° to -10°
6a	-10° to -5°
6b	-5° to 0°
7a	0° to 5°
7b	5° to 10°
8a	10° to 15°

Virginia USDA
Hardiness Zones

The zone information that you commonly see in books and magazines and on plant tags is usually about cold hardiness—the average minimum temperature range. The idea behind cold hardiness zones is to help you select plants that will likely survive winter. Keep in mind that while certain plants can often bounce back from one night at 0 degree Fahrenheit, after a week or two of 0 degrees the plants may not recover. And in Virginia there is likely a week of daytime temperatures in the 60s and 70s before the night of zero. The zone maps currently don't address these kinds of situations.

The most commonly used cold hardiness zone system is the 1990 USDA Hardiness Zone map. This map divides its zones into 5-degree subzones. (You can see the entire map online at www.usna.usda.gov/Hardzone/ushzmap.html.) This map is under revision; watch for a new version soon. According to the 1990 map, the Virginia mountains are in USDA Zones 5b and 6a, making the climate there generally a bit cooler in winter. The Piedmont runs from Zones 6b to 7a to 7b. The Eastern Shore and southeastern Virginia are Zone 7 and often Zone 8a. As you can see, all of Virginia can expect some freezing temperatures in winter.

A revised version of the USDA map was devised in 2006 by the Arbor Day Foundation (see it at www.arborday.org/media/map _change.cfm). The Arbor Day map shows how zones have changed since 1990. Arbor Day zone designations sometimes appear on plant tags for woody plants—that is, trees and shrubs. But for the most part, most publications and plant tags that you'll come across still refer to the numbers from the 1990 USDA Hardiness Zone map.

Heat zone information is not widespread yet, but knowing your heat zone may give you another dimension of knowledge about your site. For some plants, summer heat is good: It can encourage growth in tropical plants and ripen our tomatoes. Not all plants adapt well to heat: USDA Zone 3 and 4 plants, like white birches, thrive in Maine and Buffalo but struggle with the heat of Virginia. Where can you learn about heat zones? Find the American Horticulture Society's Heat Zone Map online at www.ahs.org/publications/heat_zone_map.htm.

Whether you are looking at hardiness zones or heat zones, remember that while zone designations are useful, they have limitations. For instance, even when listed as tolerant of the cold temperatures of USDA Zones 5 and 6, plants that work well in the dry cold of Colorado, like agastache, won't perform as well in the wet cold of Virginia and the rest of the East Coast. And zone ranges don't take into account the existence of microclimates in your yard—pockets of warmer or colder temperatures or areas of more or less wind. You may be able to defy your hardiness zone and grow plants labeled for USDA Zone 9 in a protected corner of your garden.

A Word about Water

Virginia gardens can receive rainfall all year, having no distinct wet and dry season. Some parts of the state have rainfall patterns that gardeners can use to their advantage.

From Winchester and Berryville to Stuarts Draft and beyond, the Shenandoah Valley of Virginia rivals the great plains of the Midwest for dryness. Averaging about 33 inches of rain per year, the Blue Ridge and Appalachian Mountains block both western and eastern weather systems from depositing much rainfall in the valley. Gardeners who live in these areas need to consider collecting spring rainwater for late-summer watering needs and plants that tolerate less moisture overall. Supplemental watering is reasonable when establishing new plants, but being attached to the end of a hose all summer quickly dulls the mind.

The mountains of southwestern Virginia, the Alleghenies, experience the heaviest rainfall in the state, about 60 inches per year. Abundant rainfall allows for a wide palette of plants, including trees that rely on even moisture. In these areas, ensuring good

Wilting and Watering

Plants only have so many ways of responding to a problem, and wilting is one common plant response to stress. Wilting could mean a vole has eaten the plant's roots, making water uptake impossible. It might signify heat stress, in which case the plant recovers once the sun and temperature go down. The plant might just need a drink of water. Too much water can also cause wilting. How can you tell the difference between too little water and two much? Here are clues:

Too little water	Too much water
Wilting through the day	Wilt in bright sunlight
Scorch on leaf edges	Yellowing leaves
Leaf curl	Leaves drop while green
Leaves lose bright color	Sudden collapse of plant
Premature flower drop	Rotting roots
Fruit shrivels and drops	Malodorous soil
Lawn shows footprints ten minutes after walking on it	Blisters on leaves

drainage is the key to avoid drowning plants that need good aeration for their roots, like boxwood, rhododendron, and lavender and other Mediterranean favorites.

Elsewhere in Virginia, the Piedmont in the broad center of the state, the Coastal Plain and Tidewater along the eastern seaboard, and northern Virginia along the Potomac receive about 45 inches of rain per year, but not always as a gentle rain. Summer thunderstorms and early fall hurricanes can drop inches of water per hour. Even in dry years these "frog stranglers" can run off and cause localized flooding rather than sinking into parched soil. Having loose organic material and good ground covers can mediate heavy rain and allow more water to soak into the soil. The driest months tend to be July and August, with hot daily temperatures

that hasten evapora-
tion of any groundwater.
Supplemental watering
may be needed for some
newly planted or moisture-
sensitive plants during these dry
periods. Fortunately, 35 to 45
inches of rain per year is usually
enough for most established woody
plants and garden plants.

Keep in mind that people tend to over-
water plants in the house and underwater plants outside. Perhaps
they think the rain and groundwater will just take care of plants
outdoors. While we have many gifts in Virginia, an even water
supply is not one of them, and attention to the needs of newly
planted trees and shrubs is crucial. A rain gauge set out while you
are watering can measure the 1 to 2 inches per week most establishing plants need.

Understanding Microclimates

What is more significant to the health of your plants than zones
and annual rainfall is how your landscape decisions (including
good siting, building good soil, and making sound plant choices)
address the temperature tolerances, drainage situations, and the
needs of plants. Microclimates—pockets of warm or cold temperatures or excessively windy areas—can work for or against you.

Temperature tolerance. A marginally hardy fig tucked into
a northeast-facing corner of the house is protected from bitter
westerly winter winds and from coming out of dormancy too
early in spring, which would make it vulnerable to late freezes. In
areas where late freezes are common, fruit trees are often planted
in north-facing areas to delay their leafing out and setting flower
buds.

Drainage. The most important factor in the winter survival of your marginally hardy plants is elimination of pockets of water that cannot drain due to frozen soil underneath. Ensuring good drainage in winter is critical. Freeze/thaw cycles—when ice in soil melts during the day and refreezes at night—often keep water from draining away from around the crown and top roots of the plant. Dryland natives, Mediterranean favorites, and other species that came from areas with dry winters cannot manage a lot of moisture when dormant. In the winter of 2007, Mexican feather grass (*Nasella tenuissima*) died where planted on flat ground where water could not drain off the plant roots. The same plant on sloping ground survived, because water moved down the hill. This plant, as well as many others, can't survive sitting in cold, wet conditions for extended periods.

How can a gardener identify these winter-wet-sensitive plants? Find out where they originated. *Nassella tenuissima* comes from Mexico. Plants from Mexico, South America, the Mediterranean, or South Africa don't generally experience wet, cold winters. You can also use the gardener's best tools: observation and experience. Agastache, sedums, dianthus, sempervivums, alpine plants, lavender, artemisia, delosperma, and *Nassella tenuissima* all need excellent drainage.

A south- or west-facing slope will be perfect for Mediterranean and other dry-climate plants that need good winter drainage and sunny afternoon heat. If your yard lacks slopes, use gravel around the crown of the plant to increase quick drainage. Better yet, build a raised gravel bed.

Plant hardiness. Gardeners and horticulturists don't yet know all the factors that affect plant hardiness, but we are learning from new plant research and from our personal experiences. For example, Karen Rexrode, owner of the late, great Windy Hill Plant Farm, talks about the beautiful pale blue-flowering *Salvia ulignosa*, a Brazilian plant that is fully hardy in Fairfax County. "We don't know what true hardiness is on some of these plants," she says. "*Setcresea* 'Purple Queen', a popular houseplant, is a tropical form of *Tradescantia* and is now surviving outside in protected spots. That's always been considered a Zone 9 plant that could not tolerate cold temps, but here it gets frozen and comes back." We may learn that these plants can survive shorts bursts of cold but that *extended* cold may kill them. As garden lecturer David Roos of the Plains puts it, "Plants don't read tags."

You may have garden space near a warm wall; in an interior courtyard; at a rocky outcrop with excellent drainage; in a frost pocket in an open, low area; and in a boggy, shaded area. For the wall and the courtyard, you can select plants that need warmer winters. The outcrop would be a perfect site for lavenders. Avoid early spring–blooming fruit trees or magnolias in the frost pocket. The boggy area will be perfect for daylilies, joe-pye weed, and goldenrod.

The issues of winter drainage, of plant hardiness, and of delaying the leafing out of frost-sensitive plants will be important when designing your gardens and experimenting with plants you want to grow successfully. Play to your strengths once you find out what they are.

Seasonal Strategies

Virginia's distinctive seasons have their delights—and their challenges. Fortunately, there are steps you can take to help your garden while you enjoy the pleasures that each season brings. Here are a few.

Spring

Spring weather is unpredictable. It can get warm in February and never get frosty again, moving right into May with ease. It can be 70 to 80 degrees for three weeks in February and then turn cold with damaging frosts through mid-May. Late frosts can turn saucer magnolias to mush and injure swelling fruit tree buds, even though daffodils and most spring bloomers like tulips, forsythia, and kerria are tough and can sit in snow without damage.

What you can do: Use old sheets, newspapers, cardboard boxes, or single or doubled lengths of spun polyester plant coverings (like Reemay) to save tender emerging plants from these late frosts. Avoid using plastic bags as coverings, as they readily transmit the cold.

Tree leaves emerge fully around the end of April in the northern areas. Peonies bloom for Memorial Day. Gardeners fret when fierce spring thunderstorms include hail, which shreds tender new leaves.

What you can do: Be ready to shield new plantings from hail with nearby buckets or cardboard boxes. Use these to protect fragile seedlings until the weather evens out.

Summer

June, July, and August are beautiful months despite periods of hot, humid, and droughty weather. Hot, humid nights cause popular perennials like lupine and delphinium to expire prematurely. Gardens at higher elevations can often include these plants, as mountain temperatures are cooler at night, but the plants will not be as long lived as those grown in the cool evenings of New England and England.

Rain gauges are useful in keeping track of rainfall affecting your plants. Thunderstorms are notoriously spotty, and a gauge will let you know if that downpour you experienced on the other side of town actually reached your garden. While daily watering of containers may be necessary, an inch or 2 of rainfall per week is enough for established plants in the ground. Observe which plants begin to wilt first, and use these as indicators of the need to water established plantings. My wilting viburnums often let me know that it's getting very dry.

A word about garden books that show daylilies blooming in conjunction with daisies, irises, roses, and phlox. Those photos are likely showing gardens in higher latitudes—such as New England or Britain—which have a longer day (meaning more sunlight), less heat, and a much shorter growing season. For example, Rochester, New York, has almost two more hours of daylight at midsummer than Winchester, Virginia, in the northernmost part of our state. In Virginia these favorite perennials bloom sequentially. We have peony season, then iris season, and then daylily season. Perennial garden fans in Virginia will find glorious plant combinations that don't rely on northern tier weather. We have an amazing array of perennials, vines, and grasses to choose from. You just need to find different garden books. Pamela Harper, the iconic Virginia gardener and photographer, has several books with exquisite plant combinations right for us. Look for her *Time-Tested Plants: Thirty Years in a Four-Season Garden*.

Fall

From mid-August into November, Virginia gardeners have a long, mild fall season with warm, sunny days and cool nights. Your first hint of the approaching fall may be wildly colorful poison ivy hugging the trunk of a nearby tree. This is my favorite time in the garden. The lengthening rays of sun shine through the narrow blades of mature ornamental grasses. Fat, sassy annuals are at their peak. Asters brighten the garden in almost every shade of pink, purple, and blue, and reliably hardy Korean mums open in soft pastels. Roses are charming now that the pesty Japanese beetles are long gone. The vivid colors of autumn bulbs, sternbergia, saffron crocus, and colchicum stand out.

After frequently dry July and August, we get lifesaving rain in September, often as the result of hurricanes. This can cause a situation that Virginia gardeners need to keep in mind: Trees, shrubs, and perennial plants get through drought by slowing their growth, sometimes drying up their leaves and, once in a while, dropping leaves altogether. Usually the plants have not died but have gone dormant. When late rains arrive, some trees and shrubs put out new leaves as if it were spring. The fresh, lush leaves are unable to harden off before the first hard freeze in October or November. When they freeze on the plant, the leaves turn brown and shrivel but don't fall off. The plants usually recover, but you may suspect that they have died. Be patient and wait until it is evenly warm the following spring before acting on your suspicion. New leaves will push off the old, dead ones. Remember that in gardening, a plant's not dead until it's warm and dead.

Avoid pruning woody plants in fall (more about pruning in chapter 4). Once there has been a killing frost, feel free to move trees, woody plants, and many perennials. Cleaning up the vegetable garden and spent annuals is a good task for a warm afternoon. You can cut stems at ground level and leave the potting mix the plants arrived in if you like. Fall is the time to plant spring bulbs: tulips, daffodils, grape hyacinth, chionodoxa, alliums, and more. You can plant bulbs until the ground freezes. The idea of the coming spring spectacular will warm you all winter.

Winter

While rare storms can dump 2 to 3 feet of snow, most southeastern and southern Piedmont areas of Virginia do not have snow cover or extended cold temperatures in winter. You can often find camellias blooming on the Eastern Shore in December and January. For western and northern areas of Virginia, the winter can be a roller coaster, with 70-degree days followed by a cold snap. Mild winter temperatures make ice storms common in all areas of Virginia. Other than avoiding tree limbs falling from the weight of the ice, gardeners can relax about ice storms. They do little damage to gardens. The exception is the habit of branches of upright conical evergreens to splay apart as ice builds. Winding rope around the evergreen so branches stay snugly in place will prevent this problem.

Snow is the gardener's friend. Under the snow, temperatures are an even 32 degrees. Harsh winds and frigid temperatures bluster above the blanket of snow, but plants remain comfortably at rest. Snow cover is not a standard feature of all areas of Virginia, but where it exists it is great for the garden. Without snow cover, gardeners can use evergreen boughs to shield favorite perennials from the bitter temperatures. Reemay, a spun polyester fabric designed as a frost cover for plants, can be used to cover raised beds if the fabric ends are adequately secured; otherwise it blows away in strong winter winds. Chopped leaves and straw can be used as mulch, allowing air space near the plants so they don't get and stay too wet.

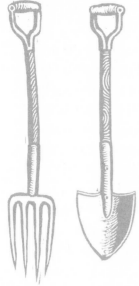

Putting a Garden Together

Choosing plants aligned with existing cultural conditions in the landscape will give you the most successful garden, one that requires the least ongoing maintenance.

When you move to a new home with existing plantings, a yard that is a blank slate, or a builder-inspired landscape, give yourself some time to discover the best and worst aspects of the place. Here are some questions to get you started:

- How do you want to use the space? What activities are important?
- Where are the shady and sunny areas in winter and summer?
- Are there great daffodils or other bulbs? If you want to see great drifts of spring daffodils from inside the house, where should you plant them?
- Do you have inside or outside views that you want to block?
- Does the backyard have a sense of privacy?
- Is the front yard welcoming or stiff?
- How does the winter wind affect the place? Is a windbreak needed?
- Are trees, shrubs, and perennials struggling or thriving?
- Are the foundation plantings appropriate or maintenance hogs?

- Can you develop some afternoon shade from the summer sun?
- Where would you put a patio and what time of day would you use it?

Become acquainted with your garden before making big decisions. Know the microclimates in your yard, and make the most of them. The idea is to go with your landscape rather than try to turn it into a wholly different place. To do this, carefully consider your yard's climate factors, soil factors, sun, and shade.

Climate Factors

Summer heat, winter warmth. Adjust summer heat by creating shade with trees or install arbors (planted with leafy vines) on the south and west of patios, decks, and indoor activity centers. Deciduous shade offers a respite from searing summer afternoon heat while allowing precious warmth and light from winter sun.

West-facing gardens. The afternoon sun is hotter than the morning sun. West-facing gardens get more intense sunlight and dry out more quickly. If these western beds are sloping, the higher parts of the slope can be perfect for sun-loving plants that hate winter wet, such as lavender.

Slopes. Frost runs downhill and settles in low, flat areas. Virginia often has late spring frosts, and frost pockets lie at the bottom of a slope. It's best to plant spring bloomers upper or mid-slope.

Another thing to remember about slopes is that they are dry because rainwater both runs downhill and evaporates up into the atmosphere. Soil on slopes can erode readily due to gravity and the wear from wind, ice, and water. Unless you terrace a slope, consider this area as dry and unstable if worked even moderately.

Slope bottoms. The bottom of slopes can be wet. Evaporation can be slow, and all the water running off the slope lingers in the soil. These areas are great places to plant hostas, Virginia bluebells, Japanese iris, and primroses but not so good for most bulbs, boxwood, rhododendrons, heathers, or Mediterranean species.

Land along creeks and streams. Small waterways may be dry in August but flood in March and April. Here you will need plants that can tolerate occasional flooding. Trees could include catalpa, dawn redwood, tupelo, bald cypress, larch, shrubby dogwoods, and river birch. Once established, many of these amazingly adaptable trees also withstand drought. (For a list of these plants, see the section "Trees and Shrubs That Can Tolerate Brief Flooding" in chapter 4.)

Soil Factors

Remember that the soil factors that we discussed in chapter 1— soil makeup, fertility, pH—will affect your plant choices. The soil next to your concrete foundation and walkways may have a higher pH (be more alkaline) than other soils in your landscape and thus be unsuitable for the traditional landscape plantings of acid-loving plants like rhododendron and azalea and holly. Boxwood or other species that tolerate more alkaline conditions make better choices in this situation.

Sun

Full sun is six hours of sun per day. Most vegetables need full sun to produce well. In the heat of summer, the sun rises at about 6:30 a.m., and many plants with an eastern exposure get their six hours by early afternoon. Roses thrive in eastern exposures. Mediterranean plants thrive in a southern or western exposure with heat and sun in the afternoon. Other plants may need supplemental watering if facing the western sun.

Sunny locations with shallow, rocky soil can be difficult to manage. Fortunately, many plants will rise to the occasion. Sedums don't require deep root space, and this makes them valuable for shallow locations (such as rocky soil or green roofs). German or bearded irises also do well. If you are brave, plant the hardy prickly pear cactus (*Opuntia* spp.). Besides having stunning yellow flowers in early summer, the prickly pear has two forms of

Some Like It Alkaline

The following is a select list of plants that will be happy in the more alkaline soil near concrete foundations, pools, walls, and walkways. And don't forget grasses. According to grasses expert Rick Darke, most ornamental grasses are indifferent to normal variations of acidity or alkalinity in soils. They should do well near foundations.

Blue oat grass (*Helictotrichon sempervirens*)

Boxwood (*Buxus* spp.)

Butterfly bush (*Buddleia davidii*)

Chaste tree (*Vitex agnus-castus*)

Crape myrtle (*Lagerstroemia indica*)

Dianthus (*Dianthus* spp.)

Elderberry (*Sambucus canadensis*)

Firethorn (*Pyracantha coccinea*)

Flowering quince (*Chaenomeles speciosa*)

Forsythia (*Forsythia* spp.)

Heavenly bamboo (*Nandina domestica*)

Juniper (*Juniperus* spp.)

Lilac (*Syringa* spp.)

Low sedge (*Carex humilis*)

Mock orange (*Philadelphus coronarius*)

Oregon grape holly (*Mahonia* spp.)

Redbud (*Cercis canadensis*)

Rose of Sharon (*Hibiscus syriacus*)

Russian sage (*Perovskia atriplicifolia*)

Spirea (*Spiraea* spp.)

Saint-John's-wort (*Hypericum* spp.)

Staghorn sumac (*Rhus typhina*)

Winter honeysuckle (*Lonicera fragrantissima*)

spines—big ones that you can see and nearly invisible glassy hairs that get into your fingers. Foxes love their fruit; you can taste it as well.

Shade

Most shade is dry shade. When planting near big trees, remember that the hydraulic ability of a tree is much more substantial than that of a perennial. A large tree can transpire (that is, move water from its roots out through its leaves) about fifty gallons of water per hour. (That's part of the reason it feels cooler under a large shade tree.) When droughts occur, smaller plants in the range of the tree's roots may not be able to get sufficient ground water to survive.

When planting under trees, don't cover up any exposed tree roots with mulch or soil. Instead, plant in the pockets between the roots. Experiment. If one type of shade plant fails, another will find the location hospitable. Consider *Epimedium* spp., *Phlox divaricata*, wild ginger (*Asarum* spp.), *Chrysogonum virginianum*, Solomon's seal (*Polygonatum* spp.), sweet woodruff (*Galium odoratum*), *Pulmonaria* spp., *Pachysandra* spp., *Helleborus foetidus*, *Euphorbia* spp., and lily of the valley (*Convallaria majalis*). You will find one or two ground covers that will spread well and cover the ground under the tree out to the edge of the tree's canopy. The ground cover provides living mulch, permits rain to soak in, reduces weeds, and keeps people from mowing and slashing exposed tree roots.

Natural woodlands have dappled shade and colonies of spring ephemerals—plants that can get the sunlight they need before tree leaves come out in April. Soils in woodlands tend to be light and fluffy because over decades leaves have decomposed into light humus. This is a great opportunity to plant early bulbs and ephemerals like mayapple (*Podophyllum peltatum*).

Not all shade is dark or deep shade. If a tree has a high canopy, considerable light may reach the understory plants. The light under the high shade of big oaks and tulip poplars, for instance, is filtered but often bright. Many shrubs, perennials, and ground covers can thrive out of the glare of the sun. Virginia sweetspire (*Itea virginica*), red buckeye (*Aesculus pavia*), spring-blooming *Kerria japonica*, and deciduous azaleas are shrubs and small trees that succeed as understory plants. Most trees tolerate the companionship, with its resulting shading of exposed roots, increased rainfall absorption, and biodiversity of soil fauna.

In contrast, there is almost no sunlight under the dense leaves of big maples. *Sarcococca hookeriana* var. *humilis* and its cousin, pachysandra, are ground covers that should do well there.

If your shade garden includes regular moisture, then you can choose from hundreds of varieties and cultivars of hosta in a dazzling array of colors, sizes, textures, and variegation patterns. The blue hostas need shade; the yellows and greens can often tolerate considerable sunshine.

Many interesting shade garden plants offer relaxation and repose rather than riotous color. Flowers are subtle and understated. Foliage is king. For example, graceful ferns and colonies of Solomon's seal can coexist with lush wild gingers (*Asarum* spp.) and jack-in-the-pulpits (*Arisaema* spp.) from China. For more ideas for shady garden areas, read *The Complete Shade Garden* by George Schenk. It's a classic, useful book.

Plant Basics

When it comes time to select plants for your garden, knowing the characteristics of different kinds of plants will help you make smart decisions. Let's look at some key characteristics.

Runner or Clumper

You already know it: Some plants run. Everyone's favorite marauder, bamboo, is reputed to run faster than my dog. The famous *Hemerocallis fulva* (known as the ditch lily, tiger lily, or tawny daylily) is a runner. This can be a good thing. If you need to cover a lot of ground, a strong-running plant may be just what you need.

Clumpers, in contrast, get fatter. The clump increases in girth over time, but it will not smoothly fill in a whole area. Most of the daylilies people fall in love with—the doubles, the pinks and apricots, the seersucker, and the picotee-edged ones—are clumpers.

Here are a few more examples:

Runner	Clumper
Liriope spicata	*Liriope muscari*
Hemerocallis fulva	*Hemerocallis flava*
Carex appalachica	*Carex pennsylvanica*
Phyllostachys (bamboo)	*Fargesia nitida* (bamboo)
Phalaris arundinacea (gardener's garters)	*Miscanthus* spp.
Arundo donax (giant reed)	*Calamagrostis* x *acutiflora* 'Karl Foerster'
peppermint	apple tree
Itea virginica (Virginia sweetspire)	*Hydrangea* spp.
Leymus arenarius (blue lyme grass)	*Nasella tenuissima* (Mexican feather grass)
Pennisetum incomptum	*Pennisetum orientale*

Deciduous or Evergreen

Without water, plants can't maintain leaves. Deciduous plants drop their leaves in fall in cold climates because winter locks up available groundwater as ice. Leaf buds on these plants have tough scales to protect them from desiccating winter winds. Deciduous trees include such favorites as maple, most oaks, ash, ginkgo, dogwood, and cherry.

Trees, shrubs, vines, grasses, and perennials that retain living leaves in the winter season are considered evergreen. In late summer and fall, their new leaves harden off, preparing for winter dormancy. Evergreen needles and leaves have a waxy covering that protects them from drying out in winter.

Most conifers are evergreen. Some have needles like pine, yew, and spruce. Chamaecyparis and arborvitae have scaled leaves that overlap, like fish scales. Some evergreens, like juniper, have stiff, scratchy awl-like leaves. Three conifers are deciduous: Larches (*Larix* spp.), dawn redwood (*Metasequoia glyptostroboides*), and bald cypress (*Taxodium* spp.) lose their needles in fall.

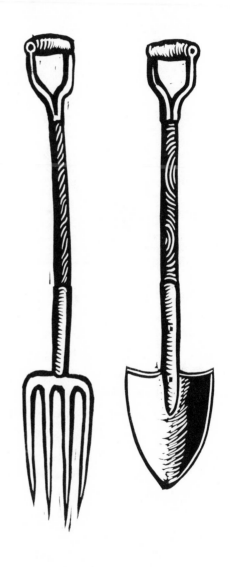

Other evergreens are called broadleaf evergreens. *Magnolia grandiflora*, and Foster's holly are broadleaf evergreens. Boxwood, rhododendrons, mahonias, camellias, and most species of holly hold their waxy leaves and are amazingly beautiful in the winter. To add to the confusion, some plant families with mostly evergreen members— like rhododendron, magnolia, and holly, also have deciduous cousins. *Ilex verticillata* is a

Monocots and Dicots

People in the horticultural trade refer to *monocots* and *dicots*. Monocots are plants that have one leaf at the time of seed germination and that have parallel leaf veins. Grass, corn, onion, iris, daylily, bamboo, and orchid are monocots. Almost every other plant is a dicot with—you guessed it—two leaves at germination. Dicot veins are not parallel but instead resemble nets. Monocots like a little extra nitrogen as they grow. As a group, dicots don't have special macronutrient requirements.

Why should you know this distinction? It will help you choose the correct herbicide. A "Grass-Go-Away"–type product is an herbicide that kills monocots. If you are trying to rid your iris bed of grass and you apply a monocot-killing herbicide, you will kill both grass and iris. A "Weed-Stop-Bothering-Me" product will affect broadleaf or dicot plants, not grasses or monocots.

very garden-worthy, deciduous holly with eye-catching berries in fall and winter. Some of the deciduous azaleas are native and have beautiful yellow, pink, and orange flowers.

Plants have evolved over long stretches of time. It's my understanding that the last four hundred years have been characterized by a beneficial climate. Even in my life I can remember colder winters and more snow. Now the climate is more variable in winter, and it's hard for us to know exactly what to expect. Imagine what it's like not only for our native plants, which evolved here with certain conditions, but for all the fantastic species brought to us from all over the world! Plants that acclimated to Virginia conditions three hundred years ago may be tested by new temperature swings and rainfall patterns.

An extended period of unusually warm weather in January 2007 brought some deciduous plants out of dormancy. My quince started blooming! Bud coverings softened and began to prepare for growth. Even the broadleaf evergreens were affected, with some of their leaf waxiness thinning. Cold weather in February followed, and many broadleaf evergreens were lightly damaged. In the winter of 1993–94, temperatures reached 15 to 24 degrees below zero in parts of Virginia. Broadleaf evergreens were badly damaged at these temperatures, though the roots were safe and most of the plants recovered over several years.

Most landscapes look good with a mix of evergreen and deciduous plants. Often people place evergreens around foundations for a uniform and formal look throughout the year. Shade trees need to provide shade only in summer, so deciduous trees are perfectly suited for that role. Many deciduous small trees and shrubs provide colorful leaves, flowers, and fruit in spring and summer, celebrating the relief from winter. Many folks cherish the fall color explosion from deciduous trees. A good balance seems to be about 30 percent evergreen to 70 percent deciduous plants. With more evergreens, things start to look gloomy.

Cool Season or Warm Season

Cool-season plants grow and flower best when temperatures are between 50 and 75 degrees. They benefit from seasonally (spring and late fall) higher levels of moisture and can withstand most frosty nights. When temperatures get high and rain becomes infrequent, these plants go into dormancy.

Pansies are a good example of cool-season plants. They can be planted in early fall when cool nights and ample rainfall help them establish. Freezing temperatures set them back but don't kill them. In early spring, moisture and sunny, warm days encourage rapid growth, and the pansies seem to double in size and bloom robustly. Once temperatures get into the 80-degree range, pansies stop flowering well and become unattractive. At this stage, most gardeners pull pansies out of the garden or cut them back to soil level. Heat-loving annual plants replace them.

Other cool-season plants include bulbs like tulips, daffodils, and crocuses native to parts of the world with long, dry seasons. Calendula, snapdragon, hellebore, bleeding heart, Oriental poppy, cabbage, lettuce, arugula, and some grasses (including calamagrostis, fescue, and helictotrichon) thrive in cool weather. These plants bloom before June 15 and take a breather during hot weather. Some will delay dormancy if you water them frequently, but this is not a low-maintenance approach.

With the exception of bulbs, cool-season plants can be moved in early spring or fall when they are actively growing but not flowering. Moving a dormant cool-season plant may kill the plant. Bulbs can be moved once their foliage cures and droops.

Warm-season plants take off slowly in spring. They are dormant in winter and thrive when temperatures range between 70 and 90 degrees. Many tolerate dry conditions well. Typically they flower after June 15. Warm-season plants include anise hyssop, butterfly bush, canna, caryopteris, chrysanthemum, cleome, corn, cucumber, gladiolus, goldenrod, miscanthus, panicum, pennisetum, pepper, portulaca, pumpkin, Russian sage, squash, tomato, and zinnia.

Warm-season plants can be divided and moved in early spring and when growing well but not when flowering. Moving them in the late fall can be risky, as they will be heading into dormancy and may not establish well in their new location before winter.

Riparian or Dryland

Some plants can live happily being flooded on occasion. Some can live with wet feet along streams and ponds, while other plants will expire in wet conditions.

Riparian species are those plants that can live in water or live with occasional flooding, like red maple (*Acer rubrum*), winterberry (*Ilex verticillata*), and dawn redwood (*Metasequoia glyptostroboides*). Some riparian plants are so adaptable that they can also survive in drought conditions, including the fringe tree

(*Chionanthus virginicus*), catalpa (*Catalpa speciosa*), and Japanese zelkova (*Zelkova serrata*).

Dryland species can be finicky. They like the right amount of water—well drained, please—and are not reliably drought tolerant. Rhododendrons and sugar maples (*Acer saccharum*) are among the dryland species sold in Virginia. Boxwood and most pines will die quickly in wet conditions.

Plants that tolerate normally dry conditions, where water deficits are frequent, make good street trees and shrubs. These include the golden rain tree (*Koelreuteria paniculata*), smoke tree (*Cotinus* spp.), and redbud (*Cercis canadensis*).

Kinds of Gardens

Virginia is a horticultural fringe area, rich in plant diversity, with many northern and southern species able to survive. When it comes to designing your garden, you have ample choices. Shrub borders can include lilacs, rugosa roses, and crape myrtles. Huge vegetable gardens including sunflowers and bramble fruits are favorites. Public and private arboretums feature a great variety of woody plants. In Virginia it's all possible.

Habitat gardens give people an opportunity to watch as raccoons, deer, butterflies, and woodpeckers visit. Native plants can play a role in habitat gardens by providing nesting places and larval food sources.

Mixed shrub borders create interesting low-maintenance gardens, in which bulbs, shrubs, small trees, flowering perennials, ornamental grasses, and ground covers grow in concert.

Collectors' gardens might have every species, variety, and cultivar of maple or hardy geranium. Dahlias fascinate some folks; daylily, herb, rose, and hosta collections are also common. Yet other gardeners limit themselves to native plants or fruit trees.

Bog gardens address a landscape problem that gives gardeners fits: a slow-draining boggy spot. Grow plants that thrive with wet feet like cardinal flower, joe-pye weed, ironweed, carnivorous pitcher plants, shrub dogwood, sweet bay magnolia, clethra, and other moisture lovers.

Dry creek gardens are ideal for landscapes that are boggy only in spring. Using good-size rocks and water-tolerant grasses like *Miscanthus gracilimus*, you can provide an attractive alternative to the muddy ruts caused by mowers. As a design feature, a dry creek is a bonus—it suggests a stream year-round.

Rain gardens are designed to slow and absorb storm-water runoff from parking lots, lawns, and roofs, water that was previously directed to storm drains and sewers. When rain gardens are used, groundwater is recharged and road and lawn chemicals and oils are prevented from washing into streams and rivers. Usually designed in good-size trenches or depressions in the landscape (so that water will collect there), rain gardens are planted with riparian species that can tolerate brief flooding. This is a good way to handle temporary storm-water runoff and enjoy very adaptable

Beware the Invasive Plant

As you search for great plants for your garden, avoid invasive plants. They can be hard to live with.

Invasive plants are certain imported species of plants that have become pests. Planted or self-seeded into areas with no natural balance to keep them in check, these plants (sometimes called exotics) overcome native species. For instance, purple loosestrife (*Lythrum salicaria*) is a showy perennial with pretty magenta flower spikes. When planted near water or even roadside ditches, purple loosestrife takes over.

Other invasive plants found in Virginia include kudzu, Asiatic sand sedge, Johnson grass, bush honeysuckles, Japanese honeysuckle, garlic mustard, common reed (*Phragmites*), tree of heaven, autumn and Russian olive, porcelain berry, and mile-a-minute vine.

The Virginia Department of Conservation and Recreation works with the Virginia Native Plant Society to distribute information about invasive plants. To get copies of fact sheets about individual invasive plants as well as other information, write to the Virginia Department of Conservation and Recreation, 1500 East Main Street, Suite 312, Richmond, VA 23219, or the Virginia Native Plant Society, P.O. Box 844, Annandale, VA 22003.

plants at the same time. For more information about rain gardens, visit a good Virginia Web site (www.dof.virginia.gov/rfb/rain-gardens.shtml) and a Wisconsin site where you can download a useful thirty-two-page manual on rain gardens for homeowners (www.clean-water.uwex.edu/pubs/pdf/home.rgmanual.pdf).

Green roofs have gained popularity in Germany and Chicago. Growing plants in frames with lightweight soil over the expanse of the roof can collect rainwater and reduce cooling expenses. Shallow-rooted succulents and some small grasses make good green roof plants.

Rose gardens are a possibility in Virginia. Heirloom and newly developed shrub roses lead the way. The old roses—like the spring-blooming damask 'Madame Hardy' and the repeating 'Stanwell Perpetual'—combine fragrance and toughness. Rose developer Dr. Griffith Buck at the University of Iowa hybridized dozens of beautiful disease-resistant shrub roses that handle the heat and humidity of Virginia with grace. Look for 'Carefree Beauty', 'Earth Song', 'Prairie Sunset', 'Hi Neighbor', and more.

There is a garden for every taste, interest, and use, from bold pool plantings to serene patio landscapes. Choose plants aligned with your activities, your sense of style, and your garden's cultural conditions.

Designing Low-Maintenance Gardens

No one wants to be tied to a home landscape with relentless chores and little joy. Some advance planning can help to cut down on the chores.

Don't get carried away. Build a landscape you can handle. Maintaining a huge lawn and individual gardens is a lot of work. So start small and build on your success.

Look at your outside space. Have a great view? Frame it with two columnar trees. Have a large open area between your house and the next? Create a visual buffer with muscular woody

plants like easy-care 10-by-10-foot elderberry plants or doublefile viburnums. By starting your garden with some big items, the landscape begins to have dimension, character, and structure.

Don't scatter. Plant in large drifts, and connect your plants together in large beds. Mowing between plants is a burden.

Consider pools of grass. The highest-maintenance and most costly feature of your landscape is your lawn. In Virginia the lawns look good in March and November and commonly brown out in the hot, dry months of summer. Water restrictions—and good sense—say that you shouldn't water lawns that will recover by themselves in late fall. Consider lawn alternatives. Another approach to consider is a generous circle or rectangle of lawn grass surrounded by big sweeps of ornamental grasses, perennial plants, shrubs, and small trees.

Remember that ground covers are key. Open ground attracts weed seeds and light permits them to germinate. Filling in spaces with plants is key to keeping weeds down. Every time you plant a new tree, plant the ground cover with it. Pachysandra and *Vinca minor* are not the only ground covers.

Think big. I use 'Goldflame' spirea under young ginkgo trees. The fall colors are complementary, and the soft, fluffy spirea is a workhorse with fresh green leaves all summer, pleasant flowers, and new (and fall) foliage of bronze and red. Spireas keep the weeds down and the mower/string trimmer away from the tree trunk. Many woody plants are low growing and adaptable as ground covers. Perennials like asters and ornamental grasses can be planted over large areas and fill in nicely. Every tree can be in a larger bed or have a suitable ground cover to eliminate having to mow and trim around it.

Use edging. Edging is helpful. Metal, brick, stone, or wood edging keeps things tidy and prevents grass from infiltrating your beds and pathways.

Install paths. Paths are crucial. You need to get from garden to the car. People will come to the door. Kids need to get to the swings. Paths make it easy. Watch to see where people walk when they are not thinking about the route. That will show you where the best paths are. Cover them with pea gravel, stone, mulch, or concrete. Gordon Hayward wrote a useful how-to book on building paths and walkways called *Garden Paths: Inspiring Designs and Practical Projects*.

Account for the mature size of foundation plants. When you choose to plant yews or junipers next to the foundation of your home, you are consigning yourself to an annual maintenance chore that will continue for as long as you live there. Yews get 30 feet tall when uninterrupted. Shrub junipers can get 10 to 15 feet tall. Those darling weeping cherries get 50 feet wide. You will be pruning them out of the way every year. By the way, concrete foundations form excellent barriers to plant roots, but roots can exploit a crack in a foundation . . . or in water pipes. Roots will not penetrate intact pipes or concrete.

Keep prickly plants away from walkways. Spruces, hollies, roses, quince, bramble fruit, Chinese chestnuts, and junipers are prickly or have prickly fruit. Placement near walkways requires pruning and cleanup to keep them from becoming a nuisance and stabbing people.

Pick pool plants carefully. Pools collect debris. When choosing plantings for pool areas, avoid trees with needles, fruit, spent flowers, or leaves that drop before the pool cover goes on in the autumn. Since people will be wearing bathing suits, avoid scratchy and thorny plants, too.

Consider parterres. Parterres are helpful. While parterres or low-hedged areas require some maintenance to keep them looking tidy, they visually contain all kinds of sprawling, leggy, or wild plants. Geometric forms have a lot of visual weight, and placing some around the house can give the space immediate character. For example, roses are favorite garden plants, but they have spindly legs. By placing roses in a square made of lavender plants or boxwood, the legs disappear and only the flowering stems show. Different low-growing plants can be used to create parterres.

Weed wisely. If you have no time to pull weeds, take the time to cut off and dispose of the seed heads of your weeds.

Fence vegetables. For all the years you will grow delicious fresh vegetables, you will always be fighting deer, woodchucks, rabbits, etc. Just give up now and fence the vegetable garden.

Fill in the space; thin out and move extras later. I once worked for a tree nursery that did landscaping. The owner/designer would set ground-covering plants at the recommended distance for their mature growth. For the next five or ten years, the clients would need to weed between those plants as they inched towards each other with glacial speed. While you weigh your options, you can choose to plant more closely and fill in the space at the beginning. Plants cost a lot less than your time and energy over those ten years.

A gardener I admire planted a new hedge of arborvitae to obscure the parking area. She planted young trees every 5 feet, clearly too close for mature growth. In a few years, the trees began to push each other. She cut down every other one, opening space for additional growth. The hedge functioned to shield her patio from the parking area from the first day.

Connect the dots. One plant here and one there is a maintenance nightmare. Plant them together, especially perennials and woodies, with consideration for their needs. Let them touch shoulders and push each other around. Swap out the ones that get overwhelmed. New combinations will appear that amaze you.

Build raised beds. We all age if we are lucky. Bending, squatting, and stooping lose their appeal in your fifties. Raised beds solve so many different problems. Be kind to yourself. Build raised beds and keep gardening into your nineties.

Mulch Myths

You will notice that in the list of low-maintenance techniques above, I haven't included a recommendation to use hardwood mulch. While the idea of applying mulch is correct, in practice mulch is usually applied badly. We are using a mistaken approach.

Some common myths about mulch:

Mulch keeps moisture in the soil. Thankfully it usually doesn't, because roots need good air exchange. If there were that much moisture in the soil, mulch would be the last thing to add. Also, when hardwood mulch is applied too thickly and dries out, it repels water, so that a light rainfall will not reach plant roots. Tiny roots work their way into the mulch to get needed water and then die as the mulch dries out.

Mulch keeps down weeds. Yes, mulch shades weed seeds so they don't germinate, but it provides a base for air-, wind-, or bird-borne seeds.

Hundreds of tons of "hardwood mulch" are used each year. This so-called mulch is not always composted wood; often it is derived from waste wood and wooden pallets that have been ground up and dyed brown. If hardwood mulch is stored in huge piles and not aerated properly, anaerobic bacteria can build in the

pile, turning the mulch sour and toxic, with a pH of 1.8 to 3.6. This problem can occur in bagged mulch too—your warning is the odor of vinegar, alcohol, or ammonia. Sour mulch will damage or kill plants.

Piling mulch up against the bark of trees and shrubs can cause suffocation. A good exchange of oxygen and carbon dioxide is necessary for the plant tissue just under the bark, at the root flare, and at the roots. Mulch can keep moisture trapped on the trunk; constantly wet bark encourages insect attacks and fungal and bacterial diseases. Mulch piled too deeply around trees and shrubs also makes good nesting sites for mice and voles. And as mulch decomposes, it heats up and can damage bark and tree roots, most of which lie in the top 8 to 12 inches of the soil.

Death from overmulching is gradual. Peeling bark on the trunk under the mulch, twig dieback, poor color and growth, and other symptoms of decline are usually visible too late to remedy the problem.

Hardwood mulch often serves as host for dog-vomit fungus, which is common and ugly but harmless. Artillery mold is more damaging. When mature, this mold shoots spores at the lightest surface in the vicinity, probably your house or car. The spores are so effective at sticking that you will rub the paint off your car before getting the spores off. Many insurance companies won't cover the damage.

This is not to say that you should never use mulch. There are good reasons to apply mulch:

- To keep mowers and string trimmers away from plants
- To keep dormant weed seeds from germinating with exposure to sunlight
- To keep lawn grass away from the base of plants
- To provide a uniform look to planting

The key is to use good material and apply it properly. It should be no more than 2 inches deep and kept well away from the trunk of any tree or shrub or the crown of perennials or grasses. Good mulch materials include finely chopped pine bark (pine fines), which does not need composting if sapwood comprises less than 10 percent of the volume; cocoa hulls; and leaf compost—they all become topsoil within a year. Pine needles, straw, and salt hay take a bit longer to decompose. Gravel mulches are good for Mediterranean plants, but other plants can suffer when the stone reflects too much heat.

Best of all, light mulch allows time for living ground covers to fill in around trees and shrubs. Living plants allow rainfall to permeate the topsoil readily. They permit good air exchange. They shade the roots, keep them cool in summer, and buffer them from winter cold. Shade prevents errant seeds from germinating, while ground covers complement the landscape, growing more lush year after year.

A common mistake among new gardeners is to buy the plants on impulse and then try to figure out what to do with them. I hope that this section has given you some tools to use before you go shopping. Now let's get into the details about plants and how you can make the most of them in your landscape.

Green Things

Trees and Woody Plants

Of all the plants in the world, the most magnificent are the trees, the bare bones of any landscape. Choosing, siting, and planting trees and woody plants will ensure that your garden has year-round beauty. We've all seen homes without trees. They appear impermanent, not settled. The fascinating and diverse array of woody plants helps to marry our homes to their environs and grace our lives.

Planting Trees

Trees are planted for the future. Over years they become more commanding in the landscape. So it's important to consider the mature size of a tree when selecting it, to plant it properly, and to select the right variety for your site. Those cute 3-foot weeping cherries in the garden center will grow to about 50 feet wide. That comes as a shock to folks who planted them right next to their front steps.

When to Plant

You can dig or move trees when they are dormant, either in the fall after the leaves drop or in the spring before the leaves emerge. In northern Virginia, the leaves usually come out fully during the last week of April. As one goes farther south, leaves emerge earlier. In mild areas or during mild winters, tree moving can continue in the winter months.

In his excellent book *Tree Maintenance*, P. P. Pirone recommends digging and planting fleshy-rooted trees like magnolia, tulip poplar, dogwood, willow, oak, and yellowwood in the spring rather than the fall for best chances of survival. He also recommends planting thin-barked trees, like river birch, in spring so they can be established before winter. Most other trees can be planted either spring or fall.

Balled and burlapped (B&B) or container-grown trees can be planted anytime you are available to water. (More about watering shortly.) B&B trees and shrubs are plants that have been dug out of the ground, either by hand or with tree spades, wrapped in burlap (or ersatz burlap) and a wire cage for easier handling, and transported either to a nursery or to you. The roots are in soil, so the trees can remain out of the ground at the nursery for months with good watering.

Some trees are sold bare-root, without any soil. They are less costly to buy and ship, but they must be planted either in the ground or in potting mix *immediately* on arrival or their bare roots will dry out and die.

Big Tree or Young Tree?

A small, young tree is less costly, easy to transport and plant in the landscape, establishes quickly, and often outpaces the growth of a larger tree, whose root mass is severely reduced when the tree is dug. Big trees take about three years to recover from being dug, moved, and replanted. In those same three years, a young tree will grow fast and strong, knitting its smaller roots into the existing landscape.

A combination of the two may be your best choice. One or two large trees will quickly provide a strong presence in your yard. You can then add smaller, younger trees that will develop over time. Interesting species and varieties of small trees are available via mail order. Because they are small enough to ship through the mail, they are also easy to plant. *Cornus mas*, a fine species of dogwood called Cornelian cherry for its fruit, is a favorite of mine. Several remarkable varieties exist, some with variegated or golden leaves. It's been easy to find them through mail-order nurseries.

You don't need to limit yourself to mail-order sources. Most nurseries carry trees in varying sizes. Young trees are typically sold in containers. Bigger trees are measured by the caliper (or diameter) of the trunk—a 1-inch tree, a 4-inch tree, and so on. Root-ball size is relative to the caliper of the tree. The root-ball on a 4-inch tree, for instance, typically weighs eight hundred pounds.

Planting Strategies

When you plant a tree, you are building the future. Young trees from the nursery can look puny in the landscape initially, yet they will grow into magnificent and massive specimens in time. Find out their mature size and allow room for them to grow. Plant them a suitable distance from your house, and give them an advantage by paying attention to good planting practices.

Examine the root-ball soil. Do not assume your new tree was grown locally or in native soil. Nurseries propagate trees in many different locations and ship them to your local nursery. Many tree nurseries are located in areas with mostly sandy soils. If the root-ball of your new tree is sandy and you are planting into a heavy Virginia clay soil, the tree will struggle and may die, though its demise will take several years.

Take the sandy soil off the roots of the tree. Don't dump it in the tree hole or use it to cover the roots. Plant the now bare-root tree immediately into your native soil. Water well. Light staking may be required the first year, but allow the tree to move slightly in the wind so it develops strength.

Plant in native soil. As you prepare the planting hole, remember: no soil amendments, please. Amending the soil in the planting hole encourages the tree roots to stay in the hole rather than venture out into native soil and get good anchorage. If you are planting in a berm, the soil should be the same throughout the berm.

In the same way, fertilizing a newly planted tree is costly to the tree and thus bad practice. Trees rarely need any fertilizer at all, and pushing new growth before root establishment in a new location leads to stress, insects, and disease.

Remove burlap and wire cages. Once you've brought the tree next to the hole you have dug, it's time to cut the wire basket, remove the ropes, nails, and peel the burlap. Using a bolt cutter, snip each wire from bottom to top in one vertical row. Once the tree is in the hole, you can just peel off the wire basket in one piece. With ropes and nails removed, you can remove the burlap by gently leaning the tree to one side, then the other.

Years ago people recommended that trees be planted with their burlap or wire cage intact so that the root-ball wouldn't dry out, "crack," and damage major roots. Some garden centers still recommend this today. Don't listen to them. Wire cages can girdle tree roots six to ten years after planting. And recent research has shown that natural burlap does not disintegrate as quickly as once thought—it can remain intact in soil for more than fifteen years, preventing tree roots from penetrating the soil in your garden. Tree roots are most plentiful in the first 12 inches of soil in wide areas around trees, up to 60 feet away for some maples. Just loosening rope ties around the trunk and folding the burlap down a few inches is not enough. The fabric needs to be removed at least one foot down—and altogether if possible.

Don't Prune at Planting Time

Recent research has determined that the old practice of pruning trees to encourage new growth at time of planting is detrimental. Let the tree settle into its new surroundings. "The young tree needs as many leaves as possible to produce food for root growth and terminal buds to make the root-promoting hormone auxin," explains Dr. Bonnie Appleton of Virginia Tech's Hampton Roads Agricultural Research and Extension Center.

Plant at the right depth. Gently excavate around the trunk of your new tree until you are able to locate three to five major roots about 4 inches out from the trunk. No more than 3 inches of soil should cover this area. Some trees have a clearly visible root flare, a zone where the bark of the tree begins to make the transition to roots. You can find it by looking for the area where the trunk flares out. This area should not be deeply buried. Plant the tree so the root flare is even with existing ground, not deeper. Only about 1 inch of soil should ever be over the flare, and mulch should not cover it. If the root flare is too deep, the bark stays too moist, stressing the tree and permitting disease and insects to flourish.

Stake only when necessary. Staking trees is necessary only in certain circumstances, such as when you are planting a tree with a lot of mass (like a full spruce or pine) or when you plant a bare-rooted tree. Trees lean when large air spaces are left in the planting hole and winds shift the weight of the tree. To help close up air spaces in the planting hole, break up clumping soil, and firm the returned soil with a digging bar while watering the tree well. Tree roots cannot cross air pockets. Trees with large root-balls don't usually need staking if well planted.

If you do stake a tree, use natural rope, bungee cord, or panty-hose. Don't use wire, plastic ties, hose-encased wire, or other inelastic materials; they can damage and girdle the tree. Go about one-third of the way up the trunk and tie the tree *loosely* to a firm stake. This prevents the tree from tipping over yet allows the tree to move in the wind, building its own strength. Remove stakes after the first year, and don't forget to remove the ties. Short-term, low staking can help a tree withstand winds until it is firmly rooted. Tight staking for too long results in weak wood development, floppy or leaning trees, and breaking trunks.

Protect against girdling. The vulnerable part of a tree is right under the bark, where water is drawn up into the tree and food is brought down. The tree's cambium is also in this area. Cambium generates new cells. If the cambium is cut or damaged all the way around the tree, the tree will die.

- Remove anything that encircles a branch or tree, such as wire from tags or stakes, chains, or plastic ties. These can cause girdling. If you need a way to attach a hammock, screw an eye-bolt into the tree; the bolt closes its hole as it gets deeper into the wood. Attach a chain to the bolt.

- Place a protective collar of hardware cloth around the base of the tree to keep rabbits, mice, or voles from girdling the tree by eating the bark and cambium in winter. Remember to remove the collar or the collar itself can girdle the tree over time.

- Use living ground covers under your trees so you won't have to use a mower or string trimmer next to the bark. Mower damage is common as people try to control grass around tree trunks. String trimmers inadvertently girdle trees as the spinning line wraps around the young tree or shrub.

Donna's Best Advice: Ground Covers and Trees

Grass is not necessarily the ideal ground cover under trees. According to consulting certified arborist Ed Milhous, some turfgrasses, like K-31 tall fescue, exude allelopathic chemicals that damage and kill trees. Finding the right ground-cover combination for any particular tree will be a chance to design attractive surroundings for your new tree and avoid negative interactions.

Look for ground covers that complement your tree. Redbud is beautifully bolstered by the deep green filigree foliage of *Helleborus foetidus*. Silvery lungworts (*Pulmonaria* spp.) brighten the ground under a weeping Japanese maple. Ginkgo is butter yellow in autumn. For a vibrant combination, surround the ginkgo with *Spiraea x bumalda* 'Goldflame', which turns bronze, red, and gold in autumn—a combination that will work at least twenty years, until the shade of the ginkgo gets too dense for the spirea. When the shrubs suffer from too much shade, they will get leggy and sparse. Cut them down and fill in with pachysandra or mahonia.

I don't encourage the use of annuals or bulbs like tulips that need yearly replacement under trees. Digging too frequently damages a tree's fine roots.

Here are ground-covering plants that will forge good partnerships with trees:

Perennials

Lily of the valley (*Convallaria majalis*)

Euphorbia (*Euphorbia* spp.)

Sweet woodruff (*Galium odoratum*)

Solomon's seal (*Polygonatum* spp.)

Liriope (*Liriope* spp.)

Pachysandra (*Pachysandra* spp.)

Comfrey (*Symphytum grandiflorum*)

Yellow-root (*Xanthorhiza simplicissima*)

Grasses

Pennsylvania sedge (*Carex pennsylvanica*)

Quaking grass (*Brizia media*)

Tufted hair grass (*Deschampsia* spp.)

Japanese forest grass (*Hakonechloa macra*)

Blue oat grass (*Helictotrichon sempervirens*)

Graybeard grass (*Spodiopogon sibericus*)

Shrubs

Glossy abelia (*Abelia* x *grandiflora*)

Climbing hydrangea (*Hydrangea anomala* subsp. *petiolaris*)

Leucothoe (*Leucothoe* spp.)

Mahonia (*Mahonia* spp.)

Creeping raspberry (*Rubus calycinoides*)

Sarcococca (*Sarcococca hookeriana* var. *humilis*)

Spirea (*Spiraea* spp.)

Deer like to clean off their antlers by rubbing them on young trees of a certain caliper, usually below 5 inches. The bark and tissue are scraped and ripped badly, sometimes fatally. If your young trees are subject to buck rubbing, you can cover the bark with plastic spirals that wind over the bark or fence off the tree with sturdy posts and fencing. This is a problem in late autumn. If you have deer, you may have this problem. Once the trees get bigger, they are safe.

Water regularly the first year. Spring-planted trees must be watered deeply and regularly through summer so that the tree builds a mass of roots in its new location. Leaves build energy stores for the tree and must have a good supply of moisture to stay functional. Water requirements are reduced for fall-planted trees, because leaves have fallen and new growth has hardened off. But thorough watering will still be needed to help the roots survive transplant shock and begin to establish in their new setting before winter locks up the groundwater as ice.

How much water is appropriate? At least an inch or 2 of water per week is needed the first year. All the effective roots are near the trunk of the tree in the root-ball. Gators, heavy-duty plastic bags that people secure around the trunk, can work effectively if regularly filled with water. The bags are secured to the trunk with Velcro straps, and the water trickles out through the bags' weep holes. Note that the bags can fold in on themselves, preventing the water from dripping out. A five-gallon bucket with a weep hole will allow water trickle into the soil. Whatever aid you use, keep that water flowing.

Keeping Trees Happy

Fortunately, trees don't require a lot of maintenance.

Fertilizing

Once you do a soil test (refer to chapter 1), you will know if you need to fertilize plants. You may need to add essential nutrients

to provide
the right bal-
ance. In gen-
eral, however, I
avoid fertilizing
trees. Living in a
part of Virginia
where rainfall is
low, I don't want
my trees to grow
more quickly or
with more lush
foliage than the
native conditions war-
rant. Most competent
arborists recommend against
fertilizing trees. Instead, allow
them to grow at their natural pace,
building slowly.

Trees with certain requirements, like acid
soil, should not be planted where alkaline conditions prevail. In Virginia alkaline conditions mostly
occur around concrete and limestone outcrops. Redbud,
lilac, and hackberry are common to Virginia and like alkaline
soils. Smoke trees (*Cotinus* spp.) will tolerate alkaline soils, as will
yellowwood, ginkgo, and Leyland cypress. Using acidifying fertilizers to counteract large volumes of concrete will be unsuccessful in
most instances.

Pruning

Use a light hand when pruning trees. Dead limbs need to be
removed for your safety. Diseased branches should be cut back to
healthy wood. Broken branches create open wounds, and cutting

the branch off appropriately will reduce the open area. Remove branches headed back into the center of the tree and low branches that hit you in the forehead or scrape against your bedroom window.

Good practice limits the amount of living wood that you take off a tree at any one time. Removing about 25 percent is enough for one year. Leave the cut-off branches near the tree while you prune so that you can see how much you have pruned; stop when you reach 25 percent. Wait until next year to trim the other branches.

Cutting just to the outside of the branch collar will allow the tree to seal the wound without extra, unnecessary effort. The surrounding tissues will swell around your cut, closing off entry to insects and disease. The branch collar is clearly visible in most maples but hard to see on some trees. Look for a slight wrinkled swelling at the base of the branch. Leaving a fat stub on the tree is not good practice. The stub will die as the tree compartmentalizes the wound, and you will have to go back later and remove the stub, causing another wound. No wound painting, please. This discredited practice traps microorganisms in the damp wound, causing more problems than it solves.

Beware of the practice of tree topping—the devastating reduction of top branches. Topping severely harms a tree. Though branches and leaves may regrow quickly, the new branches (called water sprouts) are dense and upright, structurally unsound, and congested. They support new, succulent growth susceptible to insect predation and disease outbreaks. The leaves cannot make enough food to support the mature size of the tree, and energy reserves are depleted rapidly. The sun scalds trunk and branch tissue previously shaded by the leaf canopy. According to P. P. Pirone in *Tree Maintenance*, some large trees (including sugar maples, oaks, and beeches) will not readily produce water sprouts after topping; without leaves, the tree dies.

I have seen tree-topping companies move from one end of a

street to the other, disfiguring saucer magnolias, birches, mimosas, and big maples trees in a frenzy to reduce tree size. Most tree experts agree that such trees were less dangerous before being topped. Better to remove too-large trees entirely and replace them with appropriately sized trees.

Weather Considerations for Trees and Shrubs

Hot summer weather accompanied by drought can stress your woody plants. Tree leaf edges become brown and crisp. Established trees and shrubs usually survive drought with some supplemental water.

Late-summer rain and pruning will cause woody plants to leaf out with fresh new leaves that don't have enough time to harden off for winter. When cold weather arrives, the leaves will be frozen on the plant, where they may remain until they are pushed off by new spring growth.

Ice storms can break limbs and splay branches. Gardeners with columnar plants like tall, thin boxwood or juniper can save themselves worry by wrapping the plant in a spiral of heavy twine or rope. Ice-damaged branches rarely tighten up and return to their narrow upright form.

Winter damage to broadleaf evergreens, like *Magnolia grandiflora* and boxwood, can be severe when a bitterly cold night follows warm daytime temperatures in winter. Some people promote the use of waxy antidessicants to protect against the drying effects of bitter temperatures and winter winds.

Research has shown that waxy antidessicants block the pores of leaves—preventing the leaves from transpiring during warmer days—and actually result in worse damage at temperatures below 20 degrees. Save your money.

Plant broadleaf evergreens where they receive morning sun in winter. If evergreens are sited where the afternoon sun is too warm, constructing a burlap shelter or screen to shade the evergreens from the winter sun will help. "Southwest injury" is common in Virginia, which means trees develop severe frost cracks on the southwestern side. Orchardists often paint the trunks of fruit trees white as a preventive, to reflect the afternoon sunlight.

Trees for Virginia

Many trees thrive in Virginia. What follows are recommendations for trees for certain landscape conditions.

The Grand Trees

Among the excellent large trees you can plant for your grandchildren are willow oaks (*Quercus phellos*), black gums or tupelos (*Nyssa sylvatica*), red maples (*Acer rubrum*), and ginkgos (*Ginkgo biloba*). All are majestic, beautiful, long-lived trees. They grow moderately quickly. Beeches (*Fagus* spp.) are equally wonderful but grow more slowly.

Mountain and Piedmont areas grow spruce, hemlock, oak, and tulip poplars (*Liriodendron tulipifera*). Flowering dogwood (*Cornus florida*), fringe trees (*Chionanthus virginicus*), and mountain laurel (*Kalmia latifolia*) grace many hills. Magnificent *Magnolia grandiflora* reaches 60 feet into the skies in Lynchburg and southern parts of Virginia.

The Coastal Plain borders the Chesapeake Bay and more than 3,000 miles of shoreline with salt marshes and coastal swamps, providing a rich habitat for moisture-loving trees like sweet gum and sweet bay magnolia.

Trees That Fit the House

Big trees, like maples and oaks, look wonderful at some distance from your home. Initially appearing tiny when planted next to the house, these trees are lofty and massive when mature. They dwarf homes rather than give them a sheltered look. Some people then become anxious that huge tree limbs will crash on their homes, and as a result these folks fall prey to unscrupulous tree toppers.

There are many attractive trees more proportional to most one- or two-story homes. These trees also fit well under utility lines. Dr. Bonnie Appleton of Virginia Tech's Hampton Roads Agricultural Research and Extension Center has been studying these trees since 1992. She lists them in her book, *The New York/Mid-Atlantic Gardener's Book of Lists*. Her recommendations include crape myrtle (*Lagerstroemia indica*), doublefile viburnum (*Viburnum plicatum* var. *tomentosum*), flowering apricot (*Prunus mume* 'Bonita' or 'Peggy Clark'), flowering crab apple (*Malus* spp.), fragrant snowbell (*Styrax obassia*), fringe tree (*Chionanthus virginicus*), 'Little Gem' magnolia (*Magnolia grandiflora* 'Little Gem'), paperbark maple (*Acer griseum*), redbud (*Cercis canadensis*), serviceberries (*Amelanchier arborea, A. canadensis*), and sourwood (*Oxydendron arboreum*).

Several American and Asian boxwood varieties with columnar and pyramidal growth habits offer appropriate sizes for homes instead of the more commonly used pines, spruces, and Leyland cypress. Several to consider include:

Buxus 'Green Mountain': grows 6 feet in seventeen years; dense, pyramidal

B. microphylla 'John Baldwin': grows 8 feet in fifteen years; broadly vertical

B. sempervirens 'Dee Runk': grows 15 feet in thirty-two years; narrow column

B. sempervirens 'Fastigiata': grows 10 feet in twenty-five years; narrow column

B. sempervirens 'Rotundifolia': grows 12 feet in twenty years; pyramidal

B. sinica var. *insularis* 'Wintergreen': grows 4 to 5 feet in fifteen years; loosely round

Joan Butler of Winchester is Virginia's doyenne of boxwood. Owner of a boxwood nursery for thirty years and longtime adviser to the State Arboretum of Virginia, Butler shepherds the world's largest collection of boxwood at the arboretum's Blandy Experimental Farm in Boyce, near Winchester. "Good drainage in winter is very important," says Butler.

"Boxwood are shallow rooted and benefit from about 1 inch of water per week." She warns not to go too heavy with mulch or build up soil too high under boxwood. "Don't plant them too deep or in poorly drained soil." How quickly do they grow? According to Butler, "You can expect most varieties to grow about 6 inches per year. Of course, the tiny, slow growers might grow 1 inch per year!"

Trees and Shrubs That Can Tolerate Brief Flooding

Beyond the Coastal Plain, broad areas of Virginia border runs (creeks) and rivers. Large and small trees that tolerate occasional brief flooding are among the most useful plantings in these and other areas. Some of the following trees and shrubs, once established, are versatile and tough enough to be flooded and survive drought with equanimity.

American holly (*Ilex opaca*): 15 to 40 feet (evergreen)

American sycamore (*Plantanus occidentalis*): 75 to 100 feet

Arrowwood (*Viburnum dentatum*): 6 to 15 feet

Baccharis (*Baccharis halimifolia*): 5 to 20 feet

Bayberry (*Myrica pennsylvanica*): 5 to 12 feet

Dawn redwood (*Metasequoia glyptostroboides*): 70 to 100 feet

Elderberry (*Sambucus canadensis*): 5 to 15 feet

Fothergilla (*Fothergilla gardenii, F. major*): 2 to 3 feet, 6 to 10 feet

Fringe tree (*Chionanthus virginicus*): 12 to 20 feet

Inkberry (*Ilex glabra*): 6 to 8 feet (evergreen)

Northern catalpa (*Catalpa speciosa*): 40 to 60 feet

Oriental arborvitae (*Thuja orientalis*): 18 to 25 feet (evergreen)

Pawpaw (*Asimina triloba*): 15 to 30 feet

Persimmon (*Diospyros virginiana*): 35 to 60 feet

Red maple (*Acer rubrum*): 40 to 60 feet

Spicebush (*Lindera benzoin*): 6 to 12 feet

Summersweet (*Clethra alnifolia*): 4 to 8 feet

Swamp white oak (*Quercus bicolor*): 50 to 60 feet

Tulip poplar (*Liriodendron tulipifera*): 70 to 90 feet

Willow oak (*Quercus phellos*): 40 to 60 feet

Witch hazel (*Hamamelis vernalis, H. virginiana*): 6 to 10 feet, 20 to 30 feet

These trees can stand flooding for three to five days—making them ideal for rain gardens:

American hornbeam (*Carpinus caroliniana*): 20 to 40 feet

Bald cypress (*Taxodium distichum*): 50 to 70 feet

Black gum, sour gum, tupelo (*Nyssa sylvatica*): 30 to 50 feet

Buttonbush (*Cephalanthus occidentalis*): 10 to 15 feet

Chokeberry (*Aronia melanocarpa*): 6 to 10 feet

River birch (*Betula nigra*): 40 to 70 feet

Swamp azalea (*Rhododendron viscosum*): 1 to 8 feet

Sweet bay magnolia (*Magnolia virginiana*): 10 to 25 feet

Virginia sweetspire (*Itea virginica*): 3 to 10 feet

Wafer ash (*Ptelea trifoliata*): 15 to 20 feet

Weeping willow (*Salix babylonica*): 30 to 40 feet

Winterberry (*Ilex verticillata*): 6 to 15 feet

Witherod (*Viburnum nudum*): 6 to 12 feet

Trees That Tolerate Shade

In shady, wooded home landscapes with mature trees, people often want trees on a more human scale. Consider this sample of shade-tolerant species:

Allegheny serviceberry (*Amelanchier laevis*): 15 to 25 feet

American holly (*Ilex opaca*): 40 to 50 feet

Bottlebrush buckeye (*Aesculus parviflora*): 8 to 12 feet

Hinoki cypress (*Chamaecyparis obtusa*): 25 feet

Japanese maple (*Acer palmatum*): 10 to 40 feet

Paperbark maple (*Acer griseum*): 20 to 30 feet

Pawpaw (*Asimina triloba*): 15 to 30 feet

Red buckeye (*Aesculus pavia*): 10 to 20 feet

Silverbell (*Halesia carolina*): 30 to 40 feet (container grown may be easier to establish)

Stewartia (*Stewartia pseudocamellia*): 20 to 40 feet

Sweet bay magnolia (*Magnolia virginiana*): 10 to 25 feet

Vine maple (*Acer circinatum*): 30 feet

Tree Wisdom

If you become interested in trees, I encourage you to read the work of Dr. Alex Shigo. He loved and studied trees, investigating the effects of injections, wound painting, and topping, among other practices. His book *A New Tree Biology* is fascinating.

Trees with Problems

A tree is not just a major expense, it is an investment in your future. Beautiful species and varieties will give you years of delight. A few are nuisances or inappropriate for our climate.

Black Walnut Trees

Black walnut (*Juglans nigra*) is native to Virginia. It is a fascinating tree with late leaf emergence in spring, early leaf drop in fall, and edible nuts with distinctive flavor. Many gardeners worry about growing black walnut because it is an allelopathic plant, that is, one that exudes a chemical to kill off plants that grow around it.

Black walnut exudes hydrojuglone, which in soil turns into the toxic compound juglone. All members of the walnut family (pecan, hickory, and English walnut) can exude some hydrojuglone, but black walnuts have higher concentrations. Leaves, roots, sawdust, nuts, and husks all contain the compound until they are completely decayed. A mature tree can influence sensitive plants, like tomatoes, from 50 feet away. Some of our favorites, like river birch and American holly are susceptible to this compound, but redbud, cherry, and crab apple are not affected. Other juglone-resistant plants include Oriental poppies, hosta, grape hyacinth, comfrey, Solomon's seal, and poison ivy.

Other trees exude allelopathic chemicals. Ailanthus, the tree of heaven, clears the way for its progeny with such compounds. Sugar maples and sycamores do the same.

It's Too Darn Hot Here

The following are generally not suited to the heat of Virginia.

Dwarf Alberta spruce (*Picea glauca* 'Conica') dislikes our hot, dry weather and is attacked in summer by spider mites. Typically short lived, it can revert to its nondwarf parent stock. Tougher forms of boxwood are better choices for dwarf or pyramidal evergreen plants in Virginia.

Firs (*Abies* spp.) may be grown at Virginia's cooler higher elevations. Elsewhere, rather than using firs, plant *Cephalotaxus*, the plum yew; *Cryptomeria*, the Japanese cedar; or, in full sun, some of the interesting pines.

Laburnum. Hot weather, cold injury, and susceptibility to twig blight are factors that make this tree short lived in Virginia.

Sugar maples (*Acer saccharum*) prefer the cooler and moister habitat of the northern states. For the yellow fall color of a sugar maple, try a male ginkgo.

White birches (*Betula* spp.) are attacked mercilessly by bronze birch borers. Use the river birch (*B. nigra* 'Heritage') that thrives here.

Trees That Need Special Sites

Hemlocks (*Tsuga* spp.) prefer a protected location away from wind, afternoon sun, and deer. Wooly adelgids attack hemlocks, even when the plants are sited well. Try the Japanese cedar (*Cryptomeria* spp.) instead.

Leyland cypress (x *Cupressocyparis leylandii*) is planted everywhere because of its quick growth of about 3 feet per year. It tolerates hedging well but will not survive wet feet. A favorite of bagworms, it is also attacked by several *Seridium* cankers.

Pin oak (*Quercus palustris*) must be planted in acid soil with good moisture or it will be unhappy and pallid. Lower branches droop.

Sycamores (*Plantanus occidentalis*) grow naturally with access to water, and you see them along rivers and creeks. A sycamore is a big tree that drops branches, seeds, and peeling bark. In summer sycamores can defoliate from a form of anthracnose.

Willows (*Salix* spp.) love water. The weeping willow (*S. babylonica*) is a good-size tree (20 to 40 feet with equal spread), fast growing, and will drop branches and limbs relentlessly. The wood is weak, and the trees are typically short lived. Smaller willows can be cut back annually to control size.

White pines (*Pinus strobus*) have five needles per bundle, and these soft-looking trees can grow more than a foot a year with good drainage. They suffer in boggy areas and hate salt. Place away from driveways or roads where salt is used in winter, and allow plenty of room in full sun. Don't site pines where cars will be driving over their roots, as compacted soil also stresses the trees. A stand of pines can be a great habitat for owls. You will need to provide water in drought.

Bad Ideas

Three maple trees head this list.

***Acer negundo*, *A. plantanoides*, *A. saccharinum*.** *A. negundo* is the box elder, a quick, coarse-growing tree that rots while standing and is home to gregarious box elder bugs. *A. plantanoides*, the Norway maple, is fast growing, invasive, and generates massive amounts of seed. *A. saccharinum* is not the sugar maple but the silver maple. It grows huge quickly but is short lived. Its surface roots will catch you as you walk or mow. Consider much nicer maples: The paperbark maple (*A. griseum*) is striking and versatile; *A. tartaricum* is handsome with red, winged seeds (known as samaras). Both are the perfect size for the home landscape.

Bradford pear (*Pyrus calleryanna* 'Bradford'). It is amazing that this tree continues to be sold and planted. Once heralded as the perfect tree with its lollipop shape, white (fetid) flowers in spring, and lovely fall color, the Bradford has fatal flaws With its codominant branching system, it fails at about fifteen years in the ground, when the canopy splits apart. Uprooting is also common due to the excessive leafy crown. If the stump is not removed or ground to oblivion, the pear understock will grow, thorny and vigorous. The Bradford pear was supposed to be sterile. Mating with other callery pears in the landscape, it is exceptionally invasive. Most visible in spring and fall, at every highway entrance and exit and along vast stretches of land along highways are thousands of these pears.

Chose another tree like yellowwood (*Cladastris kentuckea*) for full sun or stewartia (*Stewartia pseudocamellia*) and sweet bay magnolia (*Magnolia virginiana*) for part shade.

Mimosa (*Albizia julibrissin*). Hummingbirds love mimosas, but these trees are persistent reseeders, and the wood is brittle. Prone to *Fusarium* wilt that kills them to the ground, they then erupt with vigorous suckers. Plant annual salvias for the hummingbirds and forgo the mimosa tree.

Poplars (*Populus* spp.), especially the Lombardy poplar, are sought for their fast growth and distinctive shape. Unfortunately, they are disease and insect magnets in Virginia. For good-looking columnar trees, consider European hornbeams (*Carpinus* spp.), upright English oaks (*Quercus robur*), and columnar maples like 'Armstrong' and 'Monumental'.

Tree of heaven (*Ailanthus altissima*). Maybe it's welcome in Brooklyn, but the tree of heaven is a thug in Virginia. It grows 3 to 5 feet (or more) per year and can rapidly reach 60 feet tall. Ailanthus sends seeds everywhere, and many of those seedlings will be males that have terrible odor when flowering. This plant has no redeeming qualities except toleration of pollution and terrible planting conditions.

As Long As You Know . . .

Ash trees (*Fraxinus* spp.) have lovely fall color. White and green ash transplant easily and are quite adaptable in full sun if *not* given dry and rocky soil in which to live. Stressed trees are prone to disease and insect attack. There are many varieties to choose from; the males do not drop seed.

Black locust (*Robinia pseudoacacia*) trees grow quickly in dry, lean soils by fixing atmospheric nitrogen in their roots to create their own nitrogen supply. Brittle branches are dropped routinely, and the locust leaf miner turns the leaves brown in the latter half of the summer. Mature trees can reach 50 feet tall. The wood is rot resistant and valued for fence posts, but the locust borer can quickly destroy the tree.

Deodar cedar (*Cedrus deodara*) is among the loveliest evergreen trees, with soft branches and an elegant style. It is not reliably hardy in northern sections of Virginia, and sudden bitter cold snaps have killed all of them twice in the past sixty years. It's a tree worth replanting.

Dogwood (*Cornus florida*). Sadly, everyone's favorite spring tree, the native flowering dogwood, is susceptible to several diseases and insects, especially the fungal disease *Discula destructiva*. While most other members of the dogwood family are resistant to the disease, *C. florida* often succumbs several years after infection. Symptoms of infection include leaf retention on the lower limbs— dead leaves remain rather than fall off in fall. While some arborists recommend fungicides, timing of treatment is important, and no miracle cure has yet been found. Trees in sunny locations seem to have some resistance to *Discula*, a cool-weather fungus.

That said, Virginia songbirds rely on the fruit of *C. florida*. To help the birds, plant small, young flowering dogwoods at the edges of your property. Let them be a part of a shrub border but not a major design element. When they get the disease, they will slowly die and you can plant more for the birds. 'Appalachian Spring', a *C. florida* found in the Maryland mountains, seems to be resistant to disease. Dogwoods also get mildew that can become a problem if leaves are heavily infected. Stressed trees are commonly attacked by dogwood borers. Another native that blooms around the same time is the adaptable white-flowering fringe tree (*Chionanthus virginicus*).

Hawthorns (*Crataegus* spp.) are often planted in front of buildings where their flowers and fruit are attractive. This thorny tree is attacked by rust in Virginia's humid summers, so look for rust-resistant species like the Washington hawthorn (*C. phaenopyrum*), or *C. viridis* 'Winter King'.

Honey locust (*Gleditsia triacanthos* var. *inermis*). The honey locust is amazingly adaptable to all kinds of planting conditions and tolerates drought. The native species has harrowing thorns that can puncture tires. Serious diseases, root rots, and insects affect the thornless variety of honey locust, and though widely planted, many of these trees are in decline. It probably makes more sense to look the scholar tree (*Sophora japonica*) instead.

Osage orange (*Maclura pomifera*). A cousin of mulberry, the Osage orange is a fascinating, rot-resistant American native with unusual fruit. Described as fuzzy tennis balls or green brains, the fruit smells of citrus and has compounds that offend indoor critters including cockroaches and spiders. Previously used to fence cattle, the tree is thorny and drops fruit in the fall. The largest *M. pomifera* is at Patrick Henry's home, Red Hill, in Brookneal. It's more than 350 years old.

Princess or empress tree (*Paulownia tomentosa*). Lovely purple flowers in spring attract attention—and then generate millions of seeds in seed capsules carried on the tree through the winter. Some people plant this fast grower as an investment; it is used for coffins, bowls, and furniture in Japan.

Finally, don't forget about fruit trees. They are a delight with their spring flowers and edible fruit. Most fruit trees are short lived and require a great deal of care to prevent diseases and insect problems. Look for disease-resistant varieties. To start, grow the antique 'Arkansas Black', a wonderful apple and a great keeper. In crab apples, 'Golden Raindrops' is even Japanese beetle resistant! Most fruit trees drop fruit, and this can be a problem if they are grown near driveways and walkways. Some crab apples retain fruit that shrivels. Fruit trees are not easy, but I wouldn't be without them.

Specific to Shrubs

Shrubs usually don't get more than 15 feet high and have amazing versatility in the home landscape. They can screen unfortunate views and cover the ground with interesting foliage, colorful leaves and flowers, and berries, and do so with varied forms that enhance your landscape.

Ground-covering shrubs, like dwarf forsythia (*Forsythia bronxiensis*), sweet box (*Sarcococca hookeriana* var. *humilis*), and dwarf boxwood (*Buxus sinica* var. *insularis* 'Nana'), can fill in under trees and taller shrubs. Arching shrubs can brighten landscapes, especially the shade-loving beautyberry (*Callicarpa* spp.), with its shocking magenta berries in autumn, and the chalk white spring-flowering pearl bush (*Exchorda* x *macrantha* 'The Bride').

There are hundreds of worthy shrubs, and it will be a treat for you to explore their variety and usefulness in your garden. Here are some favorite woody plants to consider.

Boxwood (*Buxus* spp.) is a valuable shrub in the winter landscape. Deer-proof boxwood is one of the most versatile evergreens. Different varieties include small pillows, ground huggers, tall columns, vase shapes, and broad ovals. Many tolerate sun. Avoid the "English" boxwood, *B. sempervirens* 'Suffruticosa', which no longer likes to grow in Virginia. 'Justin Brouwers' is a healthy look-alike. Deciduous companions like elderberry and viburnum can shield some of the more persnickety varieties of boxwood during the hot sunny days of summer. In winter box can provide the green framework for the garden.

Heavenly bamboo (*Nandina domestica*) is a graceful, leafy, 6- to 8-foot plant reminiscent of bamboo. Vibrant red berries in fall make this evergreen a must-have in many gardens. It tolerates part shade, and you can renew it by cutting down the oldest canes in spring.

Hydrangeas come in several species of value to the Virginia gardener. *Hydrangea arborescens* 'Annabelle' is a lush, vigorous plant with huge white flower heads maturing to green. It flowers on new wood, as does the peegee hydrangea (*H. paniculata* 'Grandiflora'), with its white flowers that fade to pink, or green in the case of *H. p.* 'Limelight'.

Blue and pink mophead hydrangea (*H. macrophylla*) flowers grow from old wood. The buds develop the previous summer; deer browsing and late frosts can severely damage them. It flowers best when protected by a structure that can moderate late cold and intimidate deer. The flowers turn blue in acid soil. If hydrangeas grow next to concrete, add sulfur, pine needles, and chopped leaves to the soil to keep flowers on the blue side. Aluminum fertilizers affect hydrangea color but can accumulate to toxic levels in the soil. Use ammonium fertilizers with a light touch.

The big, white conical flowers of oakleaf hydrangea (*H. quercifolia*) form from buds set the previous year and bloom in the early summer, turning pink and rose as they mature. This is a big hydrangea with classy exfoliating bark. Plants can get 15 feet tall and wide.

Japanese andromeda (*Pieris* spp.) blooms early in white or pink cascades. Attractive and deer-proof, this shade lover is a great evergreen ground cover under trees or as a spring focal point.

Oregon grape hollies, or mahonia, are lovely evergreens. *Mahonia aquifolium* resembles blue holly but handles proximity to concrete foundations better. The leatherleaf mahonia (*M. bealei*) grows about 6 to 8 feet tall. Its elegant horizontal branch patterns make it particularly effective as a ground-covering shrub under trees. Mahonias bloom in February and March and display fragrant acid yellow flowers over dark foliage.

Russian sage (*Perovskia atriplicifolia*) shows off blue purple flowers in perfect counterpoint to the warm reds and oranges of the late-summer garden. This tough semiwoody plant can spread through new plants emerging from the roots. The winter color is silvery white—stunning against stone or evergreen backgrounds.

Viburnum (*Viburnum* spp.) This family of shrubs is large and diverse. Early-blooming dawn viburnum (*V. bodnantense*) has fragrant flowers on leggy stems. The spice varieties—*V. carlesii, V.* x *burkwoodii,* and *V.* x *juddii*—are delightfully fragrant in midspring and relatively small, reaching about 7 to 8 feet tall. The tea viburnum (*V. setigerum*) has white flowers on stems that extend about 8 feet and dazzling orange red berries in fall. *V. opulus* 'Roseum' and *V. plicatum* have snowball-like flowers with little fragrance. *V. plicatum* var. *tomentosum* cultivars include 'Mariesii', a workhorse with horizontal branching and white blooms that combine to form tiers of flowers in spring. The Prague viburnum (*V.* x *pragense*) has glossy, elongated semievergreen leaves and grows 14 by 9 feet wide. One of its parents, *V. rhytidophyllum,* is called the leatherleaf viburnum; it's a wonderful 10- to 15-foot-tall and -wide shade lover that performs well massed or as a background to showier plants. Viburnums are worthy of your exploration.

Hedges

Hedges are useful. They screen unattractive views, pool fencing, utilities, and too-close neighbors while providing green walls, backgrounds, shelter, and privacy for patio or garden. Choose hedge plants based on available space and time of year when privacy is needed. Perhaps you need to screen outside activities in summer and fall, but winter screens are unnecessary. Narrow side-yard hedges between neighbors require narrow, upright plants or trellises with vines. Large expanses can embrace a wide array of woody plants and grasses. One noteworthy hedge marked the lot line of a local development with redbuds underplanted with spicy spring-blooming viburnums and late-flowering rose of Sharon. It's lovely and effective.

If you want uniform-looking hedges to grow naturally in low-maintenance landscapes, pay attention to plant growth habits and mature size when you select plants. Inkberry holly (*Ilex glabra*) is an excellent choice for a soft, evergreen, 4- to 7-foot-tall hedge. Annual pruning is not required.

Tapestry hedges can be attractive without looking formal. To make a tapestry hedge, mix viburnums with hollies, shrubby magnolias, weigela (*Weigela* spp.), rose of Sharon, ninebark (*Physocarpus opulifolius*), boxwood, diervilla, and other woody plants to form a pleasant array of flowering and evergreen shrubs that effectively block views.

Planting and Fertilizing Shrubs

Most woody plants bought from the nursery come in containers and will be pot bound. If possible, tease the roots out of this circling growth by hand. If the roots are very woody, you will need to cut them to stop the circling.

Your shrub may have been grown in soilless potting mix. Remove as much of the mix as you can. Lightweight and porous, it will cause your plant to dry out too quickly. Other woody plants are potted and growing in finely chopped pine bark. You can leave these plants as they are.

Plant the shrub at the same level as it has been growing in the container. You may find that roots on one side are dead. This usually results from hot sun repeatedly heating one side of the pot at the nursery. Cut rather than pull dead roots.

Shallow-rooted plants like rhododendron and boxwood should not be planted deeply, as they need excellent air exchange. Water well at the rate of about 1 inch per week for the first year. Avoid fertilizers at planting time. They will be unnecessary if you have been feeding your soil.

Pruning Woody Plants

The key to good pruning is observation. Woody plants grow in different ways. Good pruning techniques can draw attention to the beauty of your plants; bad pruning can create awkward angles, vigorous water sprouts, and detrimental growth patterns.

Selective pruning can reduce the size of the plant and at the same time maintain plant health and vigor. Observe the growth habit of any woody plant—how the branches align themselves and how new growth forms. Then cut back branches to preserve a natural look and reduce the shrub's size appropriately. For example, viburnums and hollies have opposite branching. By pruning just above a set of branches, the cut branch looks more natural than leaving a big, bare stub. The plant will respond by extending those end branches rather than sending up dense twiggy growth.

Pruning Winter and Spring Bloomers

All winter- and spring-blooming shrubs flower on last year's wood and set next year's buds during June and July. Late-summer pruning removes next spring's flowers. Winter and spring bloomers should be pruned, if necessary, *right after blooming*—before mid-June when new flowers buds start developing for next year. These plants include:

Andromeda (*Pieris japonica*)

Azalea, rhododendron (*Rhododendron* spp.)

Barberries (*Berberis* spp.)

Bridal wreath spirea (*Spiraea prunifolia*)

Carolina allspice (*Calycanthus floridus*)

Cherry laurel (*Prunus laurocerasus*)

Chokeberry (*Aronia* spp.)

Clematis (*Clematis montana*)

Dogwood (*Cornus* spp.)

Flowering almond (*Prunus triloba*)

Forsythia (*Forsythia* spp.)

Fothergilla (*Fothergilla* spp.)

Fringe tree (*Chionanthus virginicus*)

Kerria (*Kerria* spp.)

Lilac (*Syringa* spp.*)*

Magnolia (*Magnolia* spp.*)*

Mock orange (*Philadelphus* spp.)

Ninebark (*Physocarpus opulifolius*)

Oakleaf hydrangea (*Hydrangea quercifolia*)

Oregon grape holly (*Mahonia* spp.)

Pearl bush (*Exchorda* spp.)

Quince (*Chaenomeles speciosa*)

Redbud (*Cercis* spp.)

Roses (heirlooms that bloom only once per year, like damask, centifolia, and *Rosa glauca*)

Tree peony (*Paeonia suffruticosa*)

Viburnums (especially the fragrant ones that bloom early, like *Viburnum carlesii*, and are not grown for berries)

Weigela (*Weigela florida*)

Winter daphne (*Daphne odora*)

Winter hazel (*Corylopsis* spp.)

Winter honeysuckle (*Lonicera fragrantissima*)

Witch hazel (*Hamamelis* spp.)

A special note on the cheery herald of spring, forsythia. The lanky stems root every 8 feet when the weight of the branch

Pruning for Winter Bark Color

Shrubby dogwoods like the *Cornus alba* 'Elegantissima' (red twig), *C. sanguinea* 'Midwinter Fire' (glowing orange twigs), and *C. sericea* 'Flaviramea' (yellow-twig dogwood) have the brightest color on new wood. Once the wood is two or three years old, it becomes a muddy brown color. These cut-and-come-again plants can be pruned each spring to about 4 to 6 inches tall. They will grow new woody stems over the summer and be bright and colorful again by winter.

Another winter beauty, *Kerria japonica*, offers welcome bright green stems in winter that never turn brown. Shade-loving kerria can be cut after blooming to control size.

brings it down to the ground. Unless you want a sprawling thicket, cut the shrub back to 3 to 4 inches from the ground after flowering. Old stems don't flower well anyway. I highly recommend the wonderful ground-covering *Forsythia viridissima* 'Bronxensis'. It is a true dwarf (about 12 inches high), flowers well, and spreads 2 to 3 feet wide. No pruning is required.

Pruning Summer Bloomers

All the summer-blooming plants can be pruned in late winter/early spring, because they flower on new (or this season's) wood. Summer bloomers include:

Annabelle hydrangea (*Hydrangea arborescens* 'Annabelle')
Beautyberry (*Callicarpa* spp.)
Blue mist shrub (*Caryopteris* spp.)
Bottlebrush buckeye (*Aesculus parviflora*)
Butterfly bush (*Buddleia* spp.)
Chaste tree (*Vitex agnus-castus*)
Crape myrtle (*Lagerstroemia* spp.)
Elderberry (*Sambucus* spp.)
Glossy abelia (*Abelia* x *grandiflora*)

Heavenly bamboo (*Nandina domestica*)

Kolkwitzia (*Kolkwitzia amabilis*)

Lavender (*Lavandula* spp.)

Peegee hydrangea (*Hydrangea paniculata* 'Grandiflora')

Pines (*Pinus*)—prune extending candles, not wood

Rose of Sharon (*Hibiscus syriacus*)

Roses (all except heirlooms and 'New Dawn')

Russian sage (*Perovskia atriplicifolia*)

Sage (*Salvia* spp.)

Saint-John's-wort (*Hypericum* spp.)

Santolina (*Santolina chamaecyparissus*)

Shrub dogwoods (*Cornus* spp.) grown for winter color

Smoke tree (*Cotinus* spp.) if pruning for good leaf color and not "smoke" flowers

Spirea species like *Spiraea* x *bumalda* that bloom in summer

Crape Myrtle Amnesty

Dr. Bonnie Appleton at Hampton Roads Cooperative Extension office has been conducting research on crape myrtles. It has been common to cut back this tree mercilessly, mainly because people choose larger cultivars than they need for their landscapes. Crape myrtles range in size from small trees to midsize shrubby forms and even low-growing bushes. Dwarf forms ('Centennial', 'Chickasaw', 'Pocomoke', and 'Victor') are mature at 3 to 5 feet tall. Bush forms run from 5 to 10 feet at maturity and include 'Acoma', 'Caddo', 'Hopi', 'Pecos', 'Tonto', and 'Zuni'. Other varieties are usually small to large trees, from 10 to 30 feet tall. Be sure that you choose the right size to avoid continuing maintenance. Crape myrtles age beautifully. All have colorful flowers and flower well without pruning.

In early spring, when the daffodils are about midway up, I cut back lavender, common sage, blue mist shrub, rose of Sharon, shrub roses (including the Knock Outs), and butterfly bush to limit size, clear away twiggy or damaged wood, and shape the new season's growth. For example, I cut back lavender to 4 to 6 inches in the shape of an inverted bowl. When it grows in summer, it maintains a beautiful rounded shape with both leaves and flowers. Rose of Sharon is attractive in a V shape, with center growth removed. All of these plants flower on the ends of their branches, not along the sides.

Pruning shrubs late in the summer, from August to October, can cause problems. New growth is stimulated by pruning and may not be able to harden off adequately before a killing frost. Cold weather will kill all that new growth and it will have wasted the plant's reserves. Take a break and avoid fall pruning.

Roses in Virginia

Can you grow roses in the humid, hot weather of the Mid-Atlantic? Yes, if you select rose varieties and cultivars that combine beauty with disease resistance. If you wish to grow hybrid tea and floribunda roses, you will need weekly fungicide sprays to control black spot and mildew. Use the Cornell mixture (see the sidebar on the next page) to control these problems. Black spot appears at about 75 degrees and tends to disappear when temperatures pass 90 degrees.

With the exception of the roses that bloom once in spring

(the old heirloom roses), "continuous bloom" roses in Virginia have three periods of good blooming: spring, summer and fall.

While most roses take about three years to become vibrant and strong, rugosa roses start out strong. These workhorses get 6 to 8 feet tall in one season. Tolerance of hot, sunny locations and disease resistance is built into them. Well-known varieties like 'Thérèse Bugnet', 'Hansa', and 'Double de Coubert' flower heavily in spring and sporadically later in summer, developing fat, rosy hips for beautiful fall display. Newer varieties, such as 'Polar Ice', bloom well all summer but don't make hips.

'Stanwell Perpetual', the only repeat blooming Scotch rose (*Rosa spinosissima*) is a charmer and, though small, belongs in any rose garden. Lacy leaves frame the white pink fragrant blooms. It resists disease well.

The late Dr. Griffith Buck, rose hybridizer of the University of Iowa, built a collection of tough, disease-resistant roses available mainly through mail order. Look for 'Carefree Beauty', 'Hawkeye Belle', 'Winter Sunset', 'Prairie Harvest', and other Buck roses.

Rose breeder Bill Radler developed the tough yellow shrub

rose 'Carefree Sunshine' and the Knock Out series of self-cleaning, disease-resistant roses. The original 'Knock Out' seems to be set back by dead-heading, so leave it alone after an early spring pruning for size control. The new 'Rainbow Knock Out' is a single, pink rose with a touch of yellow in the center—lovely.

Reliable pink roses are good blenders between other colorful plants: 'Bonica' is a pleasant, resilient pink shrub rose. It makes a nice hedge and blooms on and off all summer. 'The Fairy' is a polyantha with tiny pink blooms. 'Ballerina', a hybrid musk rose, blooms pink and then fades to white and is pretty when grown among perennials. It suffers mildly from blackspot. *R. glauca* is a charmer with distinctive blue leaves. It blooms pink once, in spring, on long arching canes without many thorns. Beautiful orange rose hips follow in autumn.

David Roos, Virginia garden lecturer and writer, recommends the China rose (*R. mutabilis*), also called the butterfly rose, for its transformational charm. It opens gold and turns to pink and rose. He likes the thornless Bourbon climber 'Zéphirine Drouhin' for reliability and toughness. Roos is particularly fond of the chestnut rose (*R. roxburghii*), also called the chinquapin rose. It's covered with prickles and gets about 10 by 12 feet tall and wide in sun, with unscented flowers and big, spiny rose hips. This rose has beautiful exfoliating gray and brown bark, so it's interesting in winter.

Maintenance of Roses

If you pick tough species and disease-resistant varieties, maintenance is easier.

Most heirloom or "old garden" roses bloom only in spring, yet their beauty and fragrance more than make up for their single flowering. Damask, centifolia, musk, noisette, gallica, and alba roses bloom for several weeks and then build for next year. Prune right after flowering.

A climbing rose should be trained to three strong stems. Flowers will form on the side or lateral branches off these main stems. The popular 'New Dawn' climber is a vigorous, apple-scented rose with serious thorns. It blooms on old wood, so don't prune it too late in the summer or in late winter.

Cutting roses back in late autumn should be limited to shortening the long canes that can whip around in winter winds. Don't cut back too far, as winter cane damage is guaranteed, and you will need to remove additional damaged stems in early spring.

Prune shrub roses carefully in spring, getting rid of dead and damaged branches, cleaning out all branches heading into the center of the rose to permit good air movement, and encouraging outward growth. When looking at the rose cane, find the bumps on the outside of the cane and make a slanting cut just above the bumps. New growth will sprout from that bump and become new branches. Because you have pruned to outward-facing bumps, the

Horticultural Heirlooms

Want to learn more about the sturdy old-fashioned or "heirloom" roses? Visit the U.S. National Arboretum in Washington, D.C. Its intoxicating collection of heirloom roses delights visitors in May and early June. Go online to www.usna.usda.gov for more information.

new branches will head to the outside of the plant and keep interior congestion to a minimum.

To control insects that can bother roses, try these tips:

- Stop rose borers from entering the canes by putting a drop of Elmer's Glue on the cut ends of the canes.
- Rose slugs are the larvae of sawflies, not caterpillars. Caterpillar remedies using Bt will not kill them, but hand picking works. Feed them to your fish.
- Japanese beetles are attracted to roses by the flowers. Cut off the blossoms during the six-week period when the beetles are mating. Japanese beetles don't swim, so you can shake them into a bucket of soapy water. Give the roses their summer feeding at this time.

Woody plants, shrubs, trees, and roses give structure, strength, and character to your garden. Many provide four-season interest, and all can be relied upon for years of extraordinary beauty.

CHAPTER FIVE

Great Perennials for Virginia Gardens

Perennial plants emerge in spring to flower, set seed (unless sterile), build energy stores through photosynthesis, and then go dormant for winter. They are expected to live more than two years. There are distinctions among perennials. Most of our garden favorites are herbaceous, nonwoody perennials that die down to the ground in winter, like peonies, daylilies, iris, phlox, and salvia. A handful of perennials have evergreen foliage, like some varieties of ferns, hardy geranium, yucca, iberis, and kniphofia. The so-called subshrubs, like lavender, Russian sage, and blue mist shrub, are thought of as perennials but are actually woody plants. (Learn more about them in chapter 4.)

When buying perennials, look for hearty growth. Nursery owners know that gardeners want to see the flowers on their plants. With so many choices, it is one way to be sure of what you are getting. But flowering is costly to a plant and it will pause after flowering to build strength. When you get it home and set it in the ground, the plant will take a breather and look tired.

Revitalization comes later. Once you know your plants well, you will want to buy them before flowering.

Plant perennials so the crown is just slightly above soil level with fine roots below. In perennials, being pot bound is not usually a problem and doesn't require cutting or detangling roots. (This is a problem with woody plants.) They are often planted in a soilless potting mix that is lighter than most soils and dries out quickly. Remove as much of the mix as possible without damaging roots. Water well to get the plants established, and hold off on fertilizers.

Perennials can best be planted in spring or early fall. Planting too late in fall can result in plants heaving out of the frozen ground because roots have not anchored them in yet.

Our winter temperature roller coaster can have a disturbing effect. Water in soils freezes in winter. During Virginia's numerous winter warm spells, water in the top layer of soil thaws and drains only to pond above the next frozen layer of soil. Chilly nights and warm days cause this effect to repeat. If the weather remains warm, lower levels of soil thaw and permit the water to drain, and all is good. More often, though, water sits just below the surface, freezing and thawing. Significant winter losses can result.

Good winter drainage can be as important as plant hardiness in determining whether plants can survive. Plants that need excellent drainage, especially Mediterranean plants, become waterlogged and stressed with winter wet. Raised or gravel beds are better for these plants.

Once people get their gardening feet solidly under them, they can plant with some idea of outcome. All gardeners experience success and failure. Failure is significant when gardeners are starting out, especially if they think their lack of skill and knowledge causes the failure. Sometimes it is just the plant. With emphasis on generating new varieties of plants for sale every year, some folks promote plants that lack vigor. If you try a plant a couple of times in different locations and it dies, it's likely a too-fragile plant.

Exceptional perennial gardens have coordinated colors and shapes blooming from spring to fall. This approach focuses on flowering rather than foliage and is challenging. In case you decide to strive for a continuous sequence of bloom, take note that the times of most difficulty are mid-June, after peonies and before daylilies, and the end of July and beginning of August.

Gems for Virginia

There are perennials that help build gardening success. This does not mean that they cannot be killed, but they are tough and forgiving. Here are some favorites:

Amsonia (*Amsonia hubrichtii*). While not as widely known as willow-leaf amsonia (*A. tabernaemontana*), this amsonia is a star. With fine foliage on 2- to 3-foot stalks, this tough native has forgettable pale blue star flowers early in spring. In late summer *A. hubrichtii* turns bright butter yellow and shines for weeks, rivaling any sugar maple for color. Insects leave it alone.

Asters (*Aster* spp.) belong in every garden. They are excellent nectar plants for beneficial insects. Blooming in colors from white to pink to blue to deep purple, asters are available in species that will tolerate shade, like the wood aster (*A. divaricatus*), and sun, like the New England aster (*A. nova-angliae*). Look for lively *A. n-a.* 'Honeysong Pink' to unify all your late summer flowers. Says Clarke County plantswoman Kathy Gibb: "'October Skies' (shorter and deeper blue) and 'Raydon's Favorite' (bright blue and muscular) are essential to any garden, blending perfectly with the really hardy chrysanthemums of any color." Both varieties are *A. oblongifolius*. If you are brave, try *A. tartaricus* 'Jindai', a Japanese native with a 4-foot-tall candelabra of pale blue flowers over low, wide leaves in early fall. This one can run slowly.

Baptisia (*Baptisia australis*). Blue flowers are hard to come by, and baptisia has them in abundance. This long-lived native perennial is strong and upright with attractive leaves all summer, growing 3 to 4 feet tall. Seedpods turn black and rattle. Having read the precautions about moving baptisia, I reluctantly attempted it. The fleshy roots came untangled, replanting was easy, and the baptisia didn't mind at all. A member of the legume family, baptisias tolerate poor soil and dry conditions, making them great for dry slopes.

Butterfly weed (*Asclepias tuberosa*) is a bright orange native plant. Butterflies drink the nectar of this beauty, so plant several around the garden.

Calamint savory (*Calamintha nepeta*) is a foot-high, valuable plant. The white-flowering form is perfectly behaved, growing where you planted it, and covered with dainty white flowers and small leaves all summer. The lilac form is pretty and seeds around everywhere. Both have a minty smell, and deer don't like them.

Catmint (*Nepeta* spp.) is a workhorse in the Virginia garden. Small-, medium-, and large-growing varieties exist, and the gray green leaves are effective blenders. With blue, pink, white, and mauve flowers and a pungent smell, catmint repels deer. 'Little Titch' and 'Select Blue' are tiny, effective front-of-the-border plants, while *N. sibirica* 'Souvenir d'André Chaudron', about 24 to 36 inches tall and 24 inches wide, will hold its own with big perennials. *N.* x *faassenii* 'Walker's Low' gets about 15 to 18 inches tall and is a good top-of-the-retaining-wall plant. 'Six Hills Giant' will reach 3 feet tall.

Catmint blooms in midspring. Once you see new leaves at the crown, you can cut the arching stems back and let new foliage and flowers emerge. This is not necessary with the tiny varieties, but without this maintenance the larger varieties can get lanky, fall over other plants, and become a nuisance. Normally this behavior would take nepeta off my list, but it blooms most of the season with blue purple flowers that bees love. It is a cousin of catnip, a reseeding annual.

Columbine (*Aquilegia* spp.). Whether you grow the native red and yellow; the striped pink, 3-foot 'Nora Barlow'; or the tiny blue *A. flabellata*, columbines provide pleasure. They are not long lived but remain in the garden by self-sowing. Good drainage will result in happier plants in sun or part shade. Ignore the leaf miner tracing lines through the leaves. The plants do. Once they set seed, you can cut columbines back to new foliage at the crown of the plant.

Coneflower (*Echinacea* spp.). The bright pink petals and orange cone of *E. purpurea* are refreshing in Virginia's midsummer season. The new melon colors are gorgeous, and I buy them every year but cannot get one through the winter. There is reputedly one growing well at Green Spring Gardens Park in Annandale. This native perennial has distinctive  relatives, including the fascinating *E. paradoxa*, with yellow petals more reminiscent of black-eyed Susan.

Cup plant, compass plant, rosinweed, and **prairie dock** (*Silphium* spp.) are among my favorite big, muscular perennials. A family of tall (5 to 7 feet) and taller (7 to 9 feet) plants, these natives have opposite leaves that form a cup to catch rainfall. There can be considerable reseeding, and each plant likes about 6 square feet of space, so plan for it.

Daylilies (*Hemerocallis* spp.). For a while I was in love with these plants. The tall, late-blooming ones, with stems 5 to 6 feet tall, got my attention. There are also night bloomers like *H. citrina* or *H. vespertina*, pale yellow and fragrant. I tried the variegated form of *H. fulva*, the ditch or tiger lily. It was pretty until it reverted to green, a victim of another unstable variegation. Place daylilies carefully; they are delicious to deer.

Euphorbia spp. are amazing. Many are blue as well as evergreen, as a few of mine are. *E. amygdaloides* var. *robbiae* is a leathery rosette of dark green leaves that spreads via creeping rhizomes, forming mats of formal-looking evergreen foliage. *E. characias* performs well in Virginia with green purple and blue-leafed forms. All have bright chartreuse flowers in early spring. Watch out for *E. cyparissias* and *E. c.* 'Fen's Ruby', a short, ferny, useful, and charming thug.

Hardy geranium (*Geranium* spp.). These true geraniums are enchanters. Low-growing pink or white *G.* 'Biokovo'; big, blousy, blue purple *G.* x *magnificum;* and the eye-catching blue of *G. himalayense* x 'Johnson's Blue' are appropriate in every type of garden. Many can be used as ground covers, and most repel deer. Good drainage is important, and sun is preferred. Look for the weaver 'Ann Folkard', with chartreuse leaves and magenta flowers appearing here and there in your garden, hiding lanky stems under other perennials.

Helianthus (*Helianthus* spp.), or perennial sunflowers, are big and robust. Several species are available at plant nurseries. Try charming *H. salicifolius* with willowlike leaves and September flowers. It holds its own with grasses and other rugged plants. One day in September, the flower buds all open at once. 'Lemon Queen' is a yellow version of the golden species.

Hosta (*Hosta* spp.). The variety of sizes, colors, and textures makes hostas valuable additions to any shade garden. They must be tasty, as deer and slugs love hosta. Look for varieties with thicker leaves to limit slug damage. There is no limiting the deer, except for well-protected planting locations and fencing.

For greater success, plant blue hostas in the shade. The greens and yellows will tolerate more sunlight but bleach out in full sun. 'Sum and Substance' is huge and chartreuse, two great qualities. The flowers of *H. plantaginea* and its hybrids have captivating fragrance.

Iris (*Iris* spp.). Blooming in April and May, the popular bearded or German iris (*I. germanica*) graces almost every home in Virginia. Colors range from chalk white to deepest purple black.

Iris Borers

The bearded iris is susceptible to iris borers. There is a curious practice of cutting back the leaves after blooming to a tidy 4 inches to prevent borer infestations. This is not an effective control, because the borer is already well into the iris rhizome. According to Ginny Spoon, owner (with her husband, Don) of Winterberry Gardens, a premier iris nursery in Cross Junction, the most effective control of iris borer is good winter cleanup—removing all the leaves, where the borer eggs have been deposited in fall. The low-dose systemic insecticide imidacloprid, sold under several names for grub control, can also help control borers when applied in spring. Adds entomology Professor Michael Raupp of the University of Maryland, "I do not like all this cutting business in the first place, and I believe it is hard on the iris to snip it back in June. I had 100 percent control of iris borers using drenches of the nematode *Steinernema carpocapsae*."

Plants need their leaf surfaces to replenish energy stores after flowering. The only value to cutting leaves short is to keep roots of newly planted rhizomes in the ground, avoiding top-heaviness. (See chapter 9 for additional strategies for dealing with iris borers.)

Three fans of leaves are required for flowering.

The Siberian iris (*I. sibirica*) is less prone to borer attack. It blooms later than bearded iris and comes with white, yellow, blue, and purple blossoms. This iris prefers sun but will tolerate a bit of shade. In a few years it will form a circle of leaves around an open center. Then it's time to lift, quarter, and replant all four divisions. A good investment!

Among my favorite irises is the variegated *I. pallida*. Its yellow and gray green leaves lift the eye with bold vertical streaks. The short Japanese roof iris (*I. tectorum*) has white or purple flowers and fans growing in waves, covering the ground (or the roof) readily. All will tolerate part shade.

Lamb's ears (*Stachys byzantina* 'Countess Helene von Stein'). Also called 'Big Ears', this variety of lamb's ears resists flowering. Normal lamb's ears flowers are OK, but clipping their unsightly flower stalks is a tedious maintenance chore. There may be one stalk of flowers per year on 'Big Ears', which is easy to forgive. This sturdy low-growing foliage plant is a soft gray green, useful in blending brighter colors in the garden. A brisk comb-through with your hands at the end of winter will help clear debris. This plant is best divided in spring.

Lysimachia spp. Many people consider these plants to be thugs, but I think some of them have excellent uses. Yellow loosestrife (*L. punctata*) is perky, a foot tall, with bright yellow flowers along the stem. It's charming in full sun but can run and overtake less vigorous companions. Put it over by the stone wall and let it run. *L. clethroides* is the gooseneck loosestrife, with graceful nodding white flowers on the top of a 2-foot-tall stem. This tough plant tolerates dry shade and is lovely in June and July. Creeping Jenny, or golden moneywort (*L. nummularia* 'Aurea'), is one of my favorites. It has chartreuse leaves and grows flat along the ground, with stems rooting as they go. A perfect ground cover, this plant gets going early in spring, growing thick enough in summer to shade out weed seeds from any sunlight but allowing bulbs and perennials to poke through easily. Tinged burgundy in winter, it is fully hardy and extremely useful, growing in both sun and shade with some moisture.

Peony (*Paeonia* spp.). There are two types of peonies: herbaceous and tree. Herbaceous peonies resemble shrubs but die back to the ground in winter. The herbaceous peony is all green stems and leaves. It has single or double pink, white, red, coral, yellow, or deep pink flowers The ants cover the buds because the peony gives them nectar in return for protection from bud-eating insects. Remember to plant peony roots just 2 inches below the

soil level. Planting too deeply or in deep shade are the main causes of poor flowering.

The tree peony is woody, but it is grafted to herbaceous peony understock. Tree peonies come in yellow, orange, true red, white, and pink. The buds are large, and the flowers have large, silky petals. When each blossom is finished, its petals flutter and fall gracefully. North Carolina gardener, author, and artist Peter Loewer recommends planting a tree peony 6 inches deeper than the graft to get the plant to root. If the tree peony dies or the graft is poor, you will begin to see herbaceous peony foliage emerge from the soil. Cut this growth back severely as long as your tree peony continues to survive. If the tree peony dies, you will have to raise the understock peony to get it to bloom, but you will have another herbaceous peony. The ants will be pleased.

Sedum (*Sedum* spp.) or stonecrops is among the most forgiving perennials. Small mat formers like *S. kamtschaticum* and large and upright *S. spectabile* 'Autumn Joy' and its many cousins flourish in most gardens. They tolerate poor, shallow soil, full sun, and drought and never whimper. White-variegated *S.* x 'Frosty Morn' is lovely but can revert, like many plants with unstable variegation. Pull out the green stems; they will overtake the plant if allowed. The big sedums have a good presence in winter when the flowers turn into brown filigree, staying upright and bold. Sedums are simple to propagate. Cut the parent plant to half its height and stick the prunings into nearby soil. They will root easily.

Red-hot poker (*Kniphofia* spp.) is a great plant with evergreen leaves. *Kniphofia* species have colorful flowers on tall spikes over narrow grassy leaves. The upright leaves are a relief from the mounding forms of most perennial plants. Flowers look like bottlebrushes and open from the bottom first. Colors range from the common red, orange, and yellow combination to 'Little Maid', a pale yellow green, and 'Ice Queen', green flowers opening white.

Rudbeckias (*Rudbeckia* spp.). You don't have to eliminate all rudbeckias from your garden just because the black-eyed Susan (*R. fulgida*) is a tedious, omnipresent rampager, spreading by seed and by stolon (great for a meadow or streamside but less welcome in the garden). Look for 5-foot-tall *R. nitida* 'Herbstonne'. With long yellow petals on a yellow green cone, it blooms for several months in summer and is a perfect hideout for the local praying mantis. Watch for large and spectacular flowers of *R. hirta* 'Prairie Sun'. Grow it from seed, as it flowers the first year. It is being sold as a perennial and is not reliably hardy. The vigorous reseeder *R. triloba* blooms in late summer and, while not long lived, will be with you forever. Think twice.

Solomon's seal (*Polygonatum commutatum*). Among the best perennials for shade, this leafy stalk with little white flowers blooming on the underside will captivate you each spring. Forming large colonies when happy, the Solomon's seal will get about 3 to 4 feet tall in most gardens. It needs a bit of moisture, and bone-dry shade will not be hospitable. The variegated forms are popular, though about two-thirds the normal size. The leaves and height make these plants welcome in any shade garden.

Using Biennials in the Garden

Biennials have a two-year life cycle. Their first year from seed is spent as a low-growing rosette of leaves. In year two, the stem elongates from the puddle of leaves, and flowers form, bloom, and set seed within a relative short time. Then the plant dies, its seeds scattered so that the species lives on. The dilemma for the gardener is deciding to have these plants taking up space in the garden for a year without flowering. Planting biennials two years in a row overcomes that problem, and you'll always have flowering plants.

Foxglove (*Digitalis purpurea*), or digitalis, is a favorite biennial. Its seed is dustlike; mulch prevents the seed from reaching welcoming soil, and leafy neighboring plants can block the light necessary for germination. Sow your own seed, dusting it on the surface of compost. Because D. purpurea is a biennial, remember that the first year's growth will be only a rosette.

There are perennial forms of digitalis. *D. parviflora* has rust red flowers, *D. grandiflora* (*D. ambigua*) and *D. lutea* are both yellow flowering and lovely. The rusty foxglove (*D. ferruginea*) is a favorite because of its caramel-colored blooms.

Honesty (*Lunaria annua*) is also called the money plant or silver dollar plant. Flowering in orchid or white, often at the same time as redbud trees in Virginia and echoing their purple limbs, this plant will thrive in open woodlands or sun. The seeds are under two green discs covering each side of the silvery interior membrane that gives the plant its common names. The shiny round translucent discs hang on the stalk long after the seeds ripen and depart and are a favorite of flower arrangers. Long in cultivation, honesty is a reliable self-seeder.

Hollyhocks (*Alcea rosea*) are tall and reminiscent of summer at the farmhouse. In Virginia hollyhocks get rust, a fungal disease that causes the leaves to be deformed. It does not seem to inter-fere with flowering, but the leaves do fall away, leaving the stalks with bare knees. Plant hollyhock among peonies or moderately sized grasses to hide the naked stems. Look for seed of *A. rugosa*, the perennial hollyhock that resists rust and powdery mildew. It features soft yellow flowers and coarse leaves.

Vines of Note

Perennial vines are useful in the garden. They create vertical interest, relieving the generally horizontal and mounded shapes of most garden plants. Like a tree, vines can screen an uninterest-ing or unpleasant view, but they do so by taking little ground space. They soften hard surfaces like walls and fences and disguise highway sound barriers. Well-placed deciduous vines create shade for warm summer afternoons yet lose their leaves to let in wel-come winter sunlight.

Some vines are chosen for their lovely flowers, like wisteria and clematis. Others, like ivy, provide a cooling backdrop. Virginia creeper and its cousin, Boston ivy, are green all summer and then shout with fiery fall color.

Some vines have a dark side. Ivy, wisteria, trumpet vine, bit-tersweet, and honeysuckle climb trees, and trees covered with vines cannot photosynthesize well and are weakened. Site these plants with care.

Among the more interesting vines available, here are some that, as perennials, will be permanent members of your garden. (Read about annual vines in chapter 7.)

Clematis (*Clematis* spp.) is a large family of plants of interest-ing shapes and colors. Clematis climbs by means of overlapping leaf stems. It cannot climb on smooth surfaces. Chicken wire, net-ting, lattice, or existing vines are needed as supports. Clematis plants are paradoxical growers: They prefer full sun on most of the vine but require shade on the roots and first foot of the vine.

Ensuring these growing conditions is awkward, because the vine is quite brittle to manipulate. The best solution comes from Longwood Gardens in Pennsylvania. Get a good-size clay pot, at least 10 inches tall. Using a screwdriver and hammer, chip away the clay to increase the size of the drainage hole. Smooth any sharp edges. Invert the pot over the planted clematis. It will climb out, seeking the light. This has two benefits besides shading the roots and crown of the vine: It keeps your feet and the string trimmer away from the base of the plant, and it keeps away rabbits (although voles can still tunnel in).

Some clematis are early bloomers, flowering on old (last year's) wood; later bloomers flower on new (this year's) wood. You can get details about the perfect pruning schedule for each type from clematis nurseries or the Internet. My pruning plan is simpler. I layer clematis. Spring, summer, and fall bloomers are planted to climb together in my garden. Every three years I cut them all down to about 4 inches from the ground after the spring bloom is over. All the dust, cobwebs, and debris of three years are disposed of, and the well-rooted vines come back quickly.

Clematis wilt is a fungal disease that kills your plant quickly. If you see that a portion of vine has wilted and blackened, prune it off and check the base of the plant. If the crown is rotted, dig up the plant and don't replant clematis in that spot. If the crown is OK, spray with the systemic fungicide benomyl according to the label instructions. It may save the plant. It may not.

The *C. montana* group is a rambunctious grower and flowers in early spring. *C. montana* 'Rubens' is pale pink with the fragrance of vanilla. Another favorite is *C. viticella* 'Betty Corning', with its recurrent, small, pale lavender downward-facing blooms with petals lilting up at the bottom. *C.* 'Guernsey Cream' is an early bloomer with a large white open flower. *C.* x *jackmanii* reveals large purple flowers in the heat of summer. Plant it nearby, because deep shades of purple are less distinct in the distance.

As far as I know, only two clematis species are pests. The fast-growing, fragrant sweet autumn clematis (*C. paniculata*) is a rampant seeder but charming if you have the space. Virgin's bower (*C. virginiana*) blooms earlier than sweet autumn clematis and has no discernible fragrance. Butterflies love it. It reseeds madly.

Climbing hydrangea (*Hydrangea anomala* subsp. *petiolaris*) is a beautiful, woody vine. While it will grow in full sun, it is best suited to shady places or a north wall, where it will be cool and serene. It climbs by means of aerial roots that grasp surfaces. While initially slow growing, this vine eventually needs strong support. It sports lovely white flowers in summer, and the vine's reddish, exfoliating bark provides winter interest. Little pruning is usually necessary.

Cross vine (*Bignonia capreolata*) is a well-behaved evergreen relative of the invasive trumpet vine. This plant's long, narrow leaves remind me of peach leaves. The early flower is red on the outside, with a yellow interior. In a bitter winter the leaves and flower buds may be frozen and drop, but leaves come back quickly in spring.

English ivy (*Hedera helix*). Thuggish behavior has made English ivy a delinquent. Its aerial rootlets from the stem will grasp flat surfaces. Exploiting cracks in window frames and foundations, English ivy has been known to take over homes and cover tree trunks in Virginia. New research has shown that ivy covering an exterior wall on a house can actually protect it from the weather. Just watch those cracks.

There are many beautiful English ivy cultivars, and not all are rampagers. Ivy is ideal for dry shade under trees. Keep the vine from climbing the tree to prevent flowering and development of fruit. Mowing in spring can keep it under control. Some nurseries sell the mature, nonvining phase of English ivy tied to a trellis. It does not climb, but it flowers and develops fruit. Watch out.

Grape (*Vitis* spp.). Grapes are vigorous growers that send out tendrils out in all directions. Grapevines need substantial support to hold up the heavy cover of leaves and fruit. Japanese beetles prey on the lush leaves, but this barely slows the development of fruit. Full sun is best for grapes, and wind protection can be important. Aligning the vines in the same direction as the prevailing winds will help.

For good fruiting, cut back the grapevines to several strong buds on lateral stems off the main trunk. Eliminate long, woody branches. Early spring is a good time to prune. Don't be surprised when water leaks from cut stems—this is normal.

Honeysuckle (*Lonicera japonica*) is the rampant, twining Japanese variety found all over Virginia. Each vine can easily grow to 30 feet in sun or shade. The fragrance in early June is luscious, but honeysuckle is difficult to control because the birds disperse its berries. The strength of this vine can deform young trees. Prune and rip out *L. japonica* relentlessly.

Nonaggressive 'Goldflame' honeysuckle (*L.* x *heckrotii*) is the offspring of *L. sempervirens*, a native vine of blue green leaves that can be semievergreen. It blooms on and off all summer with red tubular flowers with yellow on the inside. It is great in the perennial garden, even when pruned to discourage climbing. Unfortunately, it is not fragrant.

Hops (*Humulus lupulus*) is not just for making beer. It grows about 20 feet per season, dying back to the ground each winter. A plant may be male or female, but only the female flowers. A male golden-leafed form makes a refreshing curtain of foliage.

Porcelainberry (*Ampelopsis brevipedunculata*). The leaves of this vine are similar to grape leaves, though smaller and more deeply cut. The shining blue and turquoise berries are the stars—

and therein lies the problem. Birds eat the berries and spread the seed widely. Large areas have been overtaken by porcelainberry, which smothers native plants with a dense blanket of leaves and berries. It's been on the invasive plant list for a long time. It may be beautiful, but don't buy it. How about hanging turquoise jewelry on a grapevine instead?

Trumpet vine (*Campsis radicans*) flowers in yellow or orange and is a great plant for hummingbirds but not for gardens. With strong aerial rootlets, this thug grows quickly, and each flower is followed by a long pod containing a forest full of seeds. If you have an enormous space to cover and fast-moving pets, go ahead and plant trumpet vine. Just be warned that it will take over via seed and underground roots, and you'll spend years trying to get rid of it. At the very least, cut off and dispose of seedpods to restrain reseeding.

Virginia creeper (*Parthenocissus quinquefolia*) is a native vine with a five-part leaf and tiny suction-cup disks that grow from tendrils. It can climb a house or concrete wall with ease. Once established, it grows aerial roots for better anchorage. Until then, a deliberate yank will pull down 30 feet of vine attached to a brick house or tree. Radiant scarlet burgundy fall foliage graces this cousin of Boston ivy. Although its flowers don't usually show, the blue purple fruit offers a lovely contrast to the red leaves in fall. Birds love the fruit, and the leaves are food for the Pandora sphinx moth.

Winter jasmine (*Gelsemium sempervirens*) has small dark evergreen leaves with small daffodil yellow blooms that appear sometimes in December, sometimes in February. It provides welcome color in winter or early spring.

Wisteria (*Wisteria* spp.). The most beautiful wisteria I have ever seen graces the walls outside the National Gallery of Art on the Mall in Washington, D.C. The pendant purple flowers are exquisite, and the vine elegantly traces across the limestone walls. Not everyone can control this plant so well. In the warm climate of Virginia, it can be a destructive thug.

Strong supports and sharp pruners are necessary when living with wisteria. For good results in Virginia, prune summer growth and prune hard in winter. Always be sure to buy a plant that's already blooming, because some seed-borne plants won't bloom until the next millennium. Then, if your wisteria will not bloom in your garden after several years of happy vine and leaf growth, take a shovel and root prune a circle about 2 to 3 feet from the trunk. This usually does the trick.

The Asian form of wisteria has more fragrance, but the American form, *W. frutescens*, has less aggressive behavior. The violet-blue flowers appear after the first leaves and open slowly over several weeks. *W. sinensis*, the Asian form, flowers without leaves, and the flowers are short lived. Cut off seedpods and dispose of them.

Bulbs for Virginia Gardeners

When people think about perennial plants, they often overlook bulbs. But many bulbs are hardy in Virginia, bringing you colorful blooms year after year and having few maintenance requirements.

Daffodil Land

Whether you call them jonquils, daffodils, or narcissus, these perky flowers are signals of spring. Withstanding late snows and bitter winds, the bright yellow, white, pink, and orange faces of narcissus cheer us in cool spring weather. Although they are tolerant of most soil types, they dislike being wet in summer or winter soils that hold too much moisture.

Daffodil foliage needs a full six weeks after flowering to cure and photosynthesize, making food for next year's flowers. No braiding (sorry, Martha), tying with rubber bands, or chopping off the foliage, please. A grooming tip: Snap off the faded flower stalks with or without seed heads just after blooms are finished.

That alone will make the foliage look less tatty.

Plant daffodils in large drifts for easier maintenance. Generally Virginia's lawn grasses are getting unruly during the six weeks that daffodil foliage matures, and people get itchy to mow. It's easier to skirt a drift of daffodils than mow around individual bulbs. Once the foliage begins to yellow and flop, it can be mowed without damaging next spring's show.

Another great idea is to use companion plants that emerge while the daffodils are flowering or curing and shield the daffodil foliage from your view. One of my favorite companions is *Amsonia hubrichtii*. Its ferny foliage comes up while the daffodils bloom and quickly but lightly overtakes the remaining foliage. Tiny blue flowers emerge at the top of each branch. The real bonus is that the amsonia has bright

Donna's Best Advice: Daffodil Locators

You may wish to extend your daffodil drifts each fall. Unfortunately in autumn there is no foliage to mark the perimeter of your daffodil bed. An easy way to find the existing bulbs is to plant muscari, or grape hyacinth, bulbs at the edge of each year's planting. Muscari leaves emerge in fall, indicating the outline of your previous planting so that you can extend the drift without slicing existing bulbs with your shovel. An extra bonus is tiny, bright blue muscari flowers in the spring. These are a delight with daffodils. When ordering your daffodils, buy a hundred muscari and mark your edges.

butter yellow fall color. These two plants seem destined to be together, and I haven't yet seen the deer eat either. I stole the idea for this combination from Chanticleer Garden in Wayne, Pennsylvania—a garden with many ideas worth stealing

Virginia is the proud home to Brent and Becky Heath, nationally recognized daffodil and bulb purveyors. Located in Gloucester, Brent and Becky collect bulbs from all over the world to test in their gardens. They have a large mail-order clientele who enjoy both hardy and tender bulbs. Brent and Becky represent the third generation of their family working with daffodils in Gloucester. They offer great slide presentations to groups and never seem to tire of answering questions and sharing their passion and experience. Find out about tour dates and bulb availability at www.brentandbeckysbulbs.com.

Critter-proof (and especially deer-proof) daffodils are perfect for the long, mild spring season in Virginia. Brent recommends planting the early 'Rijnveld's Early Sensation' to start, followed by all the daffodils that you lust after. The last in the bloom parade is *Narcissus poeticus* var. *recurvus*; it ends the daffodil season in May.

Build your spring display by planting in the fall, starting in September. Although you can plant until the ground freezes, those daffodils will bloom late their first year. Their timing will catch up after that.

A frequent question for Brent is: My daffodil is coming up (in the fall). What should I do? "Push it back in!" Brent jokes. He adds: "This happens sometimes in Virginia. Some light compost or mulch around the new shoots will help protect them. Daffodils are pretty tough."

Daylilies and hostas can be good daffodil companions if deer are not a problem. Hardy geraniums, soft lamb's ears, and some grasses, like *Hakonechloa macra*, can also be interplanted. Cheery annual flowers or herbs such as basil can be planted to cover the dormant bulbs and summer-bare ground over them.

Brent recommends two periods of fertilization. In spring, use "a water-soluble formula such as 5-11-26 to be applied between emergence and blooming time." Using a fertilizer later in spring is wasted, since the daffodils are entering dormancy. A fall fertilizer (5-10-12 or 5-10-20) will trickle in slowly over fall and winter as daffodils are establishing their roots for next spring.

Miniature daffodils are useful in the home landscape. Many are less than 6 inches tall. They are delightful in the front or middle of garden, where emerging perennials will soon disguise their curing foliage. For the owner of a small garden, a collection of these "minis" can embody spring but not leave large areas of foliage to contend with. Please consider them.

Tulip Time

Tulips are voluptuous, but most varieties require a long, cool, damp spring to cure after blooming. Typically, Virginia gets too hot too fast in early summer to suit tulips. Again, good drainage is key. And unfortunately, the deer and the voles enjoy tulips too. It's best to think of tulips as annuals in Virginia and enjoy the fun of choosing new varieties each year. You can plant them in large bunches, as if they were in a great vase, or bed them out in Victorian and corporate fashion.

One versatile way to handle tulips is to put seven to ten of a single variety in a not-too-deep plastic pot in good potting mix. Cover with rat wire (wire mesh) or turkey grit to prevent voles and squirrels from raiding your pots. Bury the pots under finely chopped pine bark (also called pine fines) or pine needles for winter. In spring uncover your pots of tulips. You can reuse the needles or bark as a light mulch. The tulip leaves will be started up but pale. Let them green up for several days in part sun. As they come into flower, put the pots in your garden where you need a spot of bright color. When the blossoms are done, compost the plants. It's a great way to add some sparkle to the gray days of spring and brighten up some not-yet-exciting parts of your garden.

According to Brent Heath, the tulips to plant for the best

Perfect Potting

When you pot up tulips, pointy side up, be sure to put the flat side along the inside edge of the pot. The flat side indicates where a leaf will arise. The container planting will be prettier with the leaves leaning over the edge.

chance of return flowering are Darwin hybrids, single early, double early, Fosteriana, Kaufmanniana, species, and Greigii types. Experiment and see what works for you. I love 'Princess Irene', a Triumph tulip, and often a few will come back, but never in the quantities I planted initially. The variable 'Flaming Purissima' I have in a raised bed comes back in full force each spring. It is a Fosteriana.

Note that tulips coming up in your garden each year with unusually wide leaves won't bloom. They are remnants from earlier plantings and will likely never get to bloom size in our climate. Just remove them and plant a lovely group of species tulips like *Tulipa humilis* 'Eastern Star'. You will be delighted.

The Other Bulbs

Starting with snowdrops and winter aconite before winter is over, and ending with a late-fall flush of *Sternbergia lutea, Colchicum* spp., and hardy cyclamen, gardeners can enjoy flowering bulbs throughout Virginia's long growing season.

Many lovely little minor bulbs can naturalize in your garden. Try glory-of-the-snow (*Chionodoxa* spp.) in delightful blue shades in sunny or lightly shaded areas. It runs about 6 inches tall and will spread around shrubs and perennial plants.

Eranthis hyemalis, or winter aconite, is a tiny yellow-flowered bulb that blooms before forsythia. It loves growing at the foot of deciduous shade trees and will colonize if happy. The State Arboretum of Virginia in Boyce near Winchester has a lovely area where eranthis bloom each spring. A welcome sight, they precede crocuses.

Snowdrops (*Galanthus* spp.) tell us that winter will end and spring is coming. There are single- and double-flowering varieties. They seem to prefer to be lightly shaded, but they can be planted in sunny areas. They can also be moved when "in the green," in leaf, rather than waiting for dormancy.

Crocuses make a charming spectacle when planted heavily in a sunny lawn. The species forms have more longevity, but the big fat showy Dutch forms are more colorful. Use a digging fork to make holes in the lawn, pop in a crocus corm, and come back later with leaf compost to fill in the holes. It's easy to plant hundreds of little bulbs this way, and the result looks natural. Squirrels and voles like them too. Plant many.

Lily of the valley (*Convallaria majalis*) is a great ground cover for shady areas and has deliciously fragrant little white flowers in spring. The plant is toxic in all parts, which helps to keep the critters from devouring it. Definitely not an edible flower. Look for pink-flowering varieties; the current variegated form is not spectacular.

Ornithogalum spp., or star-of-Bethlehem, has two different species of use to gardeners. The shorter green and white striped form (*O. umbellatum*) is a great spring bloomer but can be invasive

Which End Up?

Planting most bulbs is easy—pointy side up works for daffodils and tulips. Both crocus and gladiolus corms have a little tip on top, and alliums have a dried mass of roots visible at the base. Some minor bulbs, like eranthis, are impossible to figure out. Fortunately, "which end up" doesn't matter thanks to geotropism—which means that bulbs can "feel" the pull of geomagnetic force and orient their growth toward the light. While it's more efficient for them to be pointed in the right direction at planting time, no need to worry. They will find their way to the sky.

if happy. The taller white form (*O. nutans*) is a tender bulb about 2 to 3 feet tall and hardy in some warmer parts of Zone 7, in southern Virginia or along the southern Coastal Plain.

The Spanish bluebell (*Endymion hispanicus*) naturalizes well throughout Virginia. Looking like a taller, loose hyacinth, it comes with pink, white, or blue bell-like flowers. The plant will seed around the garden in light to heavy shade. (Also known as *Scilla hispanica, S. campanulata,* or *Hyacinthoides hispanica.*)

Fall-blooming bulbs include the following, all hardy throughout Virginia: *Sternbergia lutea, Colchicum speciosum, Lycoris squamigera* (naked lady or magic lily), saffron crocus (*Crocus sativus*), fall crocus (*Crocus speciosus, C. pulchellus,* and others), and fall cyclamen (*Cyclamen coum* or *C. hederifolium*).

The fall bloomers are exquisitely beautiful, partly, I think, because we know what lies ahead. The colchicums remind me of raspberry water lilies, and sternbergia is like a giant daffodil-yellow crocus. The last of the bulbs, and the most charming, is the hardy cyclamen, looking every bit like a hothouse cyclamen but teeny. And then comes winter.

Not all bulbs are perennial. The exquisite Peruvian daffodil (*Hymenocallis narcissiflora*) and dahlias generally need to be lifted from the garden in fall and overwintered in a frost-free space. In some of the southern parts of Virginia, however, gardeners can overwinter the usually tender cannas and agapanthus with some added mulch. Even caladiums can make it through some mild winters. Paperwhites can be planted from late August to September for late fall bloom. They have a tiny bit of cold hardiness that permits them to withstand several frosts. Whether you plant them out in August for a fall treat or force them into bloom in the house during winter, paperwhites are not perennial here and are best composted after flowering. See chapter 7 for more about annual bulbs.

Spring Bulb Bloom Sequence

Winter aconite (*Eranthis hyemalis*); doesn't compete well;
  goes dormant after flowering

Snowdrops (*Galanthus* spp.)

Crocus (*Crocus* spp.)

Tiny iris (*Iris reticulata*); plant close for viewing

Puschkinia (*Puschkinia scilloides*); don't fertilize; good
  drainage needed

Miniature daffodils (*Narcissus* spp.)

Daffodils (*Narcissus* spp.)

Squill (*Scilla siberica*); critter-proof naturalizer; needs a little
  moisture

Glory-of-the-snow (*Chionodoxa* spp.)

Hyacinth (*Hyacinthus orientalis*)

Species tulips (*Tulipa* spp.)

Grape hyacinth (*Muscari* spp.)

Tulip (*Tulipa* spp.) other than species forms

Lily of the valley (*Convallaria majalis*); good ground cover for
  shady areas; not invasive; all parts are poisonous

Jack-in-the-pulpit (*Arisaema* spp.); fantastic plants for the
  shade garden

Wood/Spanish hyacinth (*Endymion hispanicus*)

Summer snowflake (*Leucojum aestivum*)

Star-of-Bethlehem (*Ornithogalum* spp.)

Large fritillarias (F. *persica* is dark purple; *F. imperialis* grows
  to 30 inches tall)

Spring starflower (*Ipheion uniflorum*); don't fertilize; may
  become invasive

Ornamental onion (*Allium* spp.)

Foxtail lily (*Eremurus* bungei)

Designing with Perennials

Whether you grow bulbs, biennials, vines, or old-fashioned perennial plants, perennial gardens are labor intensive. Here are my tips to make the process easier.

Think foliage. Flowers, especially perennials, bloom for about five minutes on the gardening clock. Most of the time you will be looking at plant foliage, so choose interesting foliage. Variegated or nongreen foliage can brighten an otherwise unrelenting mid-green garden.

Plant in groups or drifts. Put five hardy geraniums of the same variety next to three baptisias. You get a big show when they are in flower and can then cut back those that need it at the same time. Weeds are more visible and can easily be culled.

Look for weavers and fillers. *Geranium* 'Anne Folkard', winecups (*Callirhoe involucrata*), and 'Goldflame' honeysuckle can weave through and around perennials, bringing color to otherwise green areas. Frothy annuals like sweet alyssum or *Zinnia angustifolia* can fill in blank spaces.

Add height. Many perennials are mounders. Build contrast by adding spikes, like *Iris* spp., *Kniphofia* spp., or *Yucca* spp.

Disguise stalks. Lilies, both Oriental and Asian, need time to feed the bulb after blooming. Once the lily flower is pollinated and its petals fall off, a tall, curing stalk is visible for weeks. Plant lilies among tall plants that can hide the stalks and that don't mind being leaned on, such as woody plants like ninebark or clethra.

Know when to cut back. Many perennials renew themselves after flowering by sending up new foliage from the crown of the plant. Cut back to that new foliage when the older leaves and flowers begin to look tatty. Daylilies can be cut to the ground and will reward you with fresh new foliage. On the other hand, some flowers are followed by nutritious seed heads that make good food for birds. Echinacea and silphium will support lots of bird activity, so don't rush out to cut them down.

Relax in fall. Fall clean-up is overrated. Many perennials that are borderline in hardiness benefit from not having their crowns completely exposed to winter cold and winds. Many beneficial insects leave eggs in the perennial garden. There will be great days in early spring to start cleaning up.

Add favorite perennials to a mixed shrub border and reduce the time you spend on maintenance. Roses, evergreen and deciduous shrubs, bulbs, vines, and annuals can combine to make life beautiful and easier.

Growing Grasses

There are a great number of beautiful and useful ornamental grasses, for both sun and shade areas, and then there is lawn grass. Lawn grasses are demanding, needing liberal amounts of both sun and water. In Virginia lawns represent a huge maintenance expenditure that is rewarded by usually browning out in July, August, and September. We need to rethink our attachment to this use of land copied from British aristocrats who live in a much damper and cooler climate.

Ornamental Grasses

Carefully selected ornamental grasses give motion, texture, dimension, and vertical strength to your garden. Even on hot days, the slightest breeze will stir grass leaves, giving the gardener a sense of respite. Grasses relieve the mounding form of most perennial plants with robust vertical clumps, and their thin blades catch light beautifully, especially the low light of early morning and late afternoon. Blue grasses, like helictotrichon or blue wild rye, are distinctive counterpoints among green leaves. Variegated varieties of carex or Japanese forest grass can illuminate shady areas.

While we think of them mainly as foliage plants, grasses do flower. Cool-season grasses flower in spring or early summer; warm-season grasses bloom in the late summer and fall. Grass flowers are called inflorescences, and many are interesting and attractive. They rise above the leaves in colors and forms that bring interest to the garden. Miscanthus inflorescences are silky to the touch just before opening. Carex flowers are often spiky, while pennisetum blooms are soft and furry. Panicum inflorescences are beaded and airy. Flowers of muhly grass form a pink fog.

Select varieties that correspond well to the sun/shade, moisture conditions, and design considerations of your garden. Most gardeners buy grasses in containers from a local nursery. Plant the crown of the plant at ground level or slightly above. Grasses don't like their crown buried under soil or mulch.

Keep in mind that some grasses that behave well in lean, dry soils can spread quickly if planted in moist, nutrient-rich soils. You may want a quick-spreading plant as part of your design plan, but take a minute to think about it. To achieve a low-maintenance landscape, it's important to match the grass to the situation and the preferred outcome.

Maintenance

Ornamental grasses are low maintenance and rugged. They benefit from a gardener's neglect. Hold off on fertilizers; they grow best on lean soil. Drought resistance is common in grasses, so you'll rarely need to provide supplemental water once the grass is established. Symptoms of too much water or nutrition are lanky, floppy clumps. If your grass is in this condition, cut it back to the ground and let it resprout.

Cool-season grasses will spring to life early in spring weather and can be combed with your hand to remove spent foliage. Cut back old growth on warm-season grasses in early spring when daffodils appear. There may be bird or rabbit nests hidden within the clumping grass. Though not essential, most grasses look neater and more attractive without last year's dead leaves.

With large clumps of miscanthus or other large grasses, it's easiest to encircle the clump tightly with twine at several points and use a hedge trimmer to cut across the clump near the base. Avoid using a string trimmer for this job—cleaning up the resulting million bits of shredded grass will be daunting! Grass clumps are sometimes burned, but grass burns hot, and the flames can escape to nearby winter-dry leaves and lawns. No need to fret that warm-season grasses look dead—warm weather will encourage new leaves.

Dividing clumps is heavy work. Often the center will die out on a large stand of miscanthus or other tall grass. Lifting the entire clump is too difficult. Instead, cut out generous sections of the grass, slicing through from the dead center with a small handsaw, then lift the divisions. Planting the divisions at the same level as the older clump will offer you the best results. Divide warm-season grasses in spring. Cool-season grasses can be divided in late summer or early fall.

Resist the impulse to cut down big grasses in autumn. The warm tans of grass clumps are bold and lively in the snow, ice, wind, and birds of the winter landscape. They look especially good with conifers and other trees with winter interest, like 'Sparkleberry' holly and crab apples.

Grasses are generally deer resistant and rarely have insect problems, but rabbits relish fresh, succulent new growth. You may need to set up fencing until the grass can get big and toughens enough to fend off eager bunnies. Dried blood is supposed to repel rabbits, but it has not worked in my garden, and it attracts carnivores. More than a light sprinkling of blood will give your grass an unneeded boost of high-nitrogen fertilizer.

Ornamental grasses are important elements of the low-maintenance garden and can be used as accents, supporting players, or in major sweeps with shrubs and big perennials. There are grasses for shade or sun. Avoid the aggressive ones, like ribbon grass or blue oat grass, unless you have major ground to cover.

Shade Grasses

These grasses tolerate shade.

Autumn moor grass (*Seslaria autumnalis*)
Blue moor grass (*Seslaria caerulea*)
Golden wood millet (*Milium effusum* 'Aureum')
Golden-variegated forest grass (*Hakonechloa macra* 'Aureola')
Graybeard grass (*Spodiopogon sibericus*)
Japanese blood grass (*Imperata cylindrica* 'Red Baron')
Mondo grass (*Ophiopogon* spp.)
Northern sea oats (*Chasmanthium latifolium*)
Ribbon grass (*Phalaris arundinacea* 'Picta'); aggressive spreader
Snowy wood rush (*Luzula nivea*); needs moisture
Tufted hair grass (*Deschampsia cespitosa*)

Japanese blood grass grows in sun as well as shade, but for me it has been wimpy, not the rabid pest I was warned about. Despite my experience, it needs to be watched. Although the cultivar 'Red Baron' is not as aggressive as some tropical *Imperata*, plantsman Rick Darke warns that "there is reasonable concern that tissue culture propagation of 'Red Baron' results in a percentage of plants having the aggressive traits of the tropical phase."

Shade Sedges

Carexes, or sedges, are grasslike plants. A short poem points out the main difference between grass and sedge: "Sedges have edges and rushes are round; / Grasses have leaves that go down to the ground." Of the many species and cultivars of carex, several may be just right for your garden, either as ground covers or accent plants. This group loves part shade.

Appalachian sedge (*Carex appalachica*)
Broad-leafed sedge (*Carex plantaginea*)
Creeping broad-leafed sedge (*Carex siderostricta*)
Drooping sedge (*Carex pendula*)
Eastern star sedge (*Carex radiata*); moist shade

Foothill sedge (*Carex tumulicola*)

Fringed sedge (*Carex crinita*)

Gray's sedge (*Carex grayi*)

Miniature sedge (*Carex conica* 'Variegata')

Pennsylvania sedge (*Carex pennsylvanica*)

Rosy sedge (*Carex rosea*); especially dry shade

Silver sedge (*Carex platyphylla*)

Slender woodland sedge (*Carex digitalis*)

Spreading sedge (*Carex laxiculmis*)

Thin-fruit sedge (*Carex flaccosperma*)

Whitetinge sedge (*Carex albicans*)

Grasses and Sedges for Sun

Most ornamental grasses like sun.

Autumn flame grass (*Miscanthus* 'Purpurascens'); great fall color; rarely sets seed

Big bluestem (*Andropogon gerardii*); great fall color

Blue fescue (*Festuca glauca* varieties); cool season

Blue oat grass (*Helictotrichon sempervirens*); cool season

Blue wild rye (*Leymus arenarius*); cool season; drought/salt tolerant; can be aggressive; stabilizes slopes

Coastal switchgrass (*Panicum amarum*); all soils; drought/salt tolerant

Common rush (*Juncus effusus* varieties); hardiness varies; needs moisture

Compact pampas grass (*Cortaderia selloana* 'Pumila'); cold hardy with good winter drainage in northern and high elevations of Virginia

Feather reed grass (*Calamagrostis* x *acutiflora* 'Karl Forster'); cool season

Fiber-optics grass (*Isolepis cernua*); hardy in Zone 7 if protected

Fountain grass (*Pennisetum alopecuroides, P. orientale* spp.)

Giant feather grass (*Stipa gigantea*); cool season; needs good winter drainage

Giant reed grass (*Arundo donax*); tolerates flooding and drought

Hard rush (*Juncus inflexus* varieties); needs moisture

Indian grass (*Sorghastrum nutans* varieties)

Japanese blood grass (*Imperata cylindrica* 'Red Baron'); might be invasive

Japanese forest grass (*Hakonechloa macra*); needs good moisture

Korean feather grass (*Calamagrostis brachytrica*); tolerates part shade

Leatherleaf sedge (*Carex buchananii*)

Little bluestem (*Schizachyrium scoparium*)

Mexican feather grass (*Nasella tenuissima*); cool season

Muhly grass (*Muhlenbergia capillaris*)

Pampas grass (*Cortaderia selloana*)

Pennsylvania sedge (*Carex pennsylvanica*); needs moisture

Prairie dropseed (*Sporobolus heterolepsis*)

Purple moor grass (*Molina caerulea* subsp. *arundinacea*); cool season

Quaking grass (*Brizia maxima*); cool season; shear in late summer

Ravenna grass (*Saccharum ravennae*)

Ribbon grass (*Phalaris arundinacea*); cool season; aggressive

Silver spike grass (*Spodiopogon sibericus*); tolerates part shade

Silver/maiden grass (*Miscanthus* spp.)

Switchgrass (*Panicum virgatum* varieties)

Tufted hair grass (*Deschampsia cespitosa*); cool season; tolerates part shade

Variegated sedge (*Carex morrowii* and *C. oshimensis* varieties); tolerates part shade

A caution about miscanthus grasses: In the long, warm, moist summers of Virginia, some miscanthus varieties can flower and ripen seed. This allows those varieties to naturalize in the local area, outside of the garden, displacing native grasses. You may have noticed this in your neighborhood, wondering why anyone would plant so many miscanthus behind a guardrail. According to Rick Darke, grasses expert and author of the must-have book *The Encyclopedia of Grasses for Livable Landscapes*, in cooler climates the varieties 'Gracillimus', 'Variegatus', and 'Zebrinus' flower late and seeding is not a problem. "In warmer parts of Virginia, they set copious fertile seed."

Darke has noted that the attractive German cultivars of miscanthus developed by Ernst Pagels flower early and so can be expected to seed around in the extended fall season of Virginia. These include 'Aethiopien', 'Altweibersommer' ('Indian Summer'), 'Bronceturm' ('Bronze Tower'), 'Flamingo', 'Graziella', 'Grosse Fontäne' ('Large Fountain'), 'Juli' ('July'), 'Kaskade' ('Cascade'), 'Kleine Fontäne' ('Little Fountain'), 'Kleine Silberspinne' ('Little Silver Spider'), 'Malepartus', 'Nippon', 'Positano', 'Pünktchen' ('Little Dot'), 'Roland', 'Roterpfeil' ('Red Arrow'), 'Silberspinne' ('Silver Spider'), 'Silberturm' ('Silver Tower'), 'Undine', 'Wetterfahne' ('Weathervane'), and 'Zwergelefant' ('Dwarf Elephant'). If you wish to grow these beauties, remove the seed heads when they are most beautiful in early fall. "I typically try to encourage gardeners to consider using *Panicum virgatum* and *Panicum amarum* as alternatives to miscanthus in the Mid-Atlantic area, especially when gardening near natural areas," says Darke.

Lawn Grasses

What turfgrass mixes do well in Virginia's challenging climate? The best mixes combine cool- and warm-season grasses, says Mike Goatley, a turf specialist with the Virginia Tech Cooperative Extension office in Blacksburg.

Cool-season grasses for Virginia include Kentucky bluegrass, tall fescue, fine-leaf fescue, and perennial rye. These grasses look so lush and green from October through May.

Warm-season grasses include other tall fescues (there are more than one hundred varieties), new hybrids of Texas and Kentucky bluegrasses, Bermuda grass, zoysia, and St. Augustine and centipede grasses in the warm southeastern part of Virginia. K-31 is often spoken of as a great lawn grass. It is one of the warm-season tall fescues; its only down-side is its high mowing requirement.

Many folks think of lawn grass as both a minimal and a necessary approach to landscaping. Lawns actually require a high level maintenance to look good. They need sun and lots of water, liming, mowing, dethatching, drilling, mowing, reseeding, mowing, raking, and mowing. Trees, shrubs, and ground covers are much less costly in terms of water, maintenance, time, and other resources.

Lawn Alternatives

You might consider getting out from under the burden of so much lawn. Large planting beds with small trees, flowering shrubs, ornamental grasses, bulbs, and perennials provide one alternative. Another is using native grasses in place of lawn grasses, an approach that is gaining in popularity. Native grasses are shorn once per year, in spring, and then allowed to grow all season. Most are relatively short and don't look weedy. Mike Goatley is following research on the potential of blue grama grass, a low, native bunching grass that germinates quickly and tolerates humidity.

Prairie dropseed (*Sporobolus heterolepsis*) has been used on some lawns in the Mid-Atlantic with great success. This grass is a clump former that will lightly seed around. Clumps slowly broaden, getting more handsome each year, and the 12- to 16-

inch grass arches in swirling sweeps, turning orange in the fall. Only one mowing in the spring is required.

Dr. Lou Verner of the Virginia Department of Inland Fisheries has been doing work on wildlife habitat and native plant landscapes. He suggests mixes of short clump-forming fescues for more naturalistic lawns. He also recommends sedge lawns. Sedges (*Carex* spp.) cannot be heavily walked on "but make a loose carpet that can easily be interplanted with bulbs and other flowering plants," Verner says. Some folks use ivy, liriope, partridgeberry, wintergreen, moss phlox (*Phlox subulata*), and pachysandra as lawn alternatives. Verner recommends planting at half the recommended distance for quicker coverage. I agree.

Coping with Bermuda Grass

Bermuda grass, also called wire grass, is a nuisance for gardeners when it intrudes on ornamental planting beds, infests vegetable beds, and sends its wiry stolons over walks and pathways. This warm-season grass is aggressive and hard to kill.

Shawn Askew, turf scientist at Virginia Tech, is an expert on methods to rid your home landscape of Bermuda grass. He offers three strategies, though he is quick to point out that no method is quick or easy. Professional turf companies will work on this problem for you, or you can tackle it yourself.

Method 1. Using two ounces of the herbicide Ornamec 170 (fluazifop) and one-and-a-half ounces of the herbicide Turflon Ester (triclopyr) per gallon of water, spray the Bermuda grass three times, three weeks apart, starting when the grass starts to green up in spring. That's around mid-May in the western areas; it might be February in southeastern parts of Virginia. It's not necessary to wet the grass; a quick pass over the plant with the spray will suffice. With this method you can cover about 1,000 square feet per gallon and prevent serious damage to your cool-season grasses. Askew suggests spraying in square sections so you can treat the same area each time. You might add food coloring so you can see where you have already sprayed. If you spray at too high a concentration for either herbicide or apply too much as you spray, you will damage your remaining lawn grasses. This process is repeated in fall, when the cool-season grasses start to perk up after the hot summer, with three sets of spraying three weeks apart. (Eastern areas would start in September, running through the end of October. Western areas should start in August and end by October 1.)

Askew readily admits that you will initially see no changes after all this effort, and that can lead to dismay. Take heart. Stolon development of the grass is reduced, and it will be sufficiently injured to die over the winter. In year two, when you do this again, only 10 to 50 percent of the Bermuda grass will be alive. In year three, 1 to 3 percent will remain. It's perfectly OK to pull actively growing Bermuda grass during this process. Just don't get discouraged.

Method 2. Complete renovation of lawn areas is another approach. In this case, superconcentrated Roundup is used at the rate of four to five ounces per gallon of water. All vegetation is killed. Everything will be brown. Askew suggests doing this in sections over a couple of years, since it has to be done in the fall to kill the warm-season Bermuda grass. Water well and wait two weeks after spraying to see if anything is recovering. That will bring up sprouts from the remaining hidden stolons of the Bermuda grass. A week after the second application, you can put down your new grass seed. Early September is a good time to put down grass seed because of that month's warm days and cool nights for germination.

Method 3. Using a sod cutter, remove infested portions of the lawn. Visible stolons can be removed and new sod laid down. Replacement sod will not have Bermuda grass, but Bermuda sprouts may emerge between the sod strips. Any sprouts that infiltrate the new sod can be pulled or spot treated. Askew suggests getting a sponge pen or dish-soap holder, attaching it to a broom handle, and using the same concentration of Roundup as method 2 for spot treatment when plants are at low infestation levels. (One ounce per cup of water would be about the same.) The sponge application will prevent spray drift and keep damage of desirable plants to a minimum. The sponge technique also works well in ornamental planting beds to fight Bermuda grass without the labor of hand pulling.

With the abundance of beautiful grasses and lawn alternatives, the opportunity to reduce maintenance chores associated with lawns is something to consider. Our climate makes the bright green lawns of England or even of Pennsylvania difficult to attain and costly in effort and resources. Please consider reducing the amount of land in turfgrass and use some of the exciting and attractive alternatives.

CHAPTER SEVEN

Great Annuals

Once when I was rhapsodizing about perennial gardens, a lifelong gardener whom I admire stopped me and asked, "What is wrong with annuals?" After a long pause, I responded that you had to buy them every year. "But they flower all summer!" she replied. She was right. Ever since then I have been planting annuals in new and old varieties and colors with delight and abandon. Annuals bloom all season, filling in happily as perennials flower and fade. Annuals can be supporting players or stars, ground covers or massed accents.

Annuals are defined as plants that go from seed to flower to ripening seed then death in one growing season. But when we use the term "annuals" in Virginia, we often refer to true annuals, half-hardy perennials, perennials that are killed by our cold winters, and tropical plants that we buy and plant each summer.

So let's sort out our terms. True annuals include cleome and marigolds. Half-hardy perennials include 'Prairie Sun' rudbeckia and *Salvia farinacea*, plants that will sometimes make it through the winter but more often will not. Perennials killed by winter cold include angelonia and snapdragons. Bananas and *Brugsmansia* are tropical plants.

Pansies, calendulas, and other cool-season annuals fade rapidly as temperatures rise. Snapdragons perform well in the early and late-summer periods when cooler evening temperatures prevail. Dahlias often wait for the cooler evenings of late August and

September to bloom well. Brugsmansia loves heat, as do *Zinnia angustifolia*, castor bean, and canna.

Our summers often include extended rain-free periods. July and August are hot and steamy, and the sun drives moisture from the soil. Hot, humid nights and temperatures regularly over 85 degrees Fahrenheit give a tropical feel to summer. Virginia gardeners are used to supplying supplemental water to plantings in late summer, but community water-use restrictions often occur during these periods. You may want to consider installing rain barrels so that you can stockpile abundant spring rains to help the garden through dry summer days. Otherwise, reconsider the annual plants that you use. Plants that require lots of water to thrive belong in water gardens.

A to Z of Annuals

With these thoughts in mind, your choice of annuals to celebrate growing seasons becomes clearer. The following sturdy annuals will perform well once established, without fuss or constant deadheading:

Ageratum (*Ageratum houstonianum*). Whether you chose the short floss flower or the 2-foot 'Tall Cut Wonder', ageratum has graced Virginia gardens for many years. Tufts of dusty blue at the edge of any garden are a delight and flowers last well into fall. New varieties have a purple tinge.

Ammi majus looks like a more delicate Queen Anne's lace, great for the cutting garden and a valuable blender between colorful neighbors or tired perennials. Grow from seed each year.

Angelonia angustifolia is a member of the snapdragon family. This deer-resistant plant from the West Indies is not a true annual, but dies here because it is killed by the cold. Flowering in deep purple, bicolored blue or purple with white, or chalky white, it flowers on spires like a minifoxglove. Good in pots with good drainage.

Bidens or **beggar's tick** (*Bidens ferulifera*) has sunny yellow tiny daisylike flowers that are produced all summer over ferny foliage. It is a ground-covering annual, spreading wide and not tall. In drought, deer will go after it but usually they leave it alone.

Buenos Aires verbena (*Verbena bonariensis*) is a scrim plant. Small mauve flowers on 3-foot stems dance over low foliage on this mint family relative. Butterflies love it. This verbena often survives winter in Virginia, and it also reseeds.

Celosia (*Celosia* spp.) are exciting in the garden. If you want bold color and plants that can fill in the spaces between perennials or grasses, think celosia. Either as feathery fronds (*C. plumosa*) of deep pink, claret, and orange or strange shapes of cockscombs (*C. cristata*) in bright yellow or red, the myriad colors, sizes and shapes can add zest to the garden. Plant several in a group, as single blooms can look awkward.

Coleus (*Solenostemon scutellarioides*) has come a long way. There are varieties for sun and shade, with little, streaked, ruffled, huge, terra-cotta, burgundy, and chartreuse leaves. An easy foliage plant, its sun tolerance is gauged by leaf thickness. Thin leaves brighten shady areas. Coleus resents cold weather so don't jump into the season too quickly with this plant. These are great plants for containers. Pinch out flower buds to keep leaf color from fading.

Cosmos (*Cosmos* spp.). The stiff branching habit of yellow-orange *C. sulphureus* keeps it upright, while the pinks and whites of *C. bipinnatus* get lanky and lean over as summer advances.

Evolvulus glomeratus is a soft mounder with true blue flowers. Blue is a hard flower color to find, because most flowers shift toward mauve and lavender undertones. Here the color is clear and bright.

Fan flower (*Scaveola aemula*) is in the mauve range of blue, and the plant spreads horizontally to great effect. Native to Australia, it loves our hot summer climate.

Four-o'clock (*Mirabilis jalapa*) is a charming reseeding annual. It's easy to grow and an excellent plant for attracting hummingbirds and evening moths.

Geraniums (*Pelargonium* spp.) are interesting tropical plants loving hot and dry areas. They are great for summer containers. White, pink, orange, and red flowers are cheery. 'Mrs. Henry Cox' has beautiful and versatile variegated foliage with teal, brown burgundy, and cream markings. Scented geraniums are also valuable in containers. Look for the furry peppermint geranium, with its extraordinary horizontal growth habit and great fragrance.

Globe amaranth is a short plant with lots of impact. Flowers come in white, pink, strawberry red, and the best, magenta—always a useful color in the garden. They keep blooming over the summer and flowers can be dried.

Heliotrope. Fragrant of vanilla and romance, heliotrope has dark green leaves and is lovely when massed near brighter flowering plants.

Marigolds (*Tagetes* spp.) are the ultimate in cheery annuals, bright orange, and yellow in stripes, tufts, or chubby flowers. The foliage fragrance repels some critters (including most deer), but the cheer this compact plant brings to the vegetable garden is unmistakable. There are different species and varieties, including a 6- to 9-footer that is reputed to repel nematodes.

Melampodium paludosum. I resist planting this annual, not because it reseeds readily, but due to the killer yellow color of the flowers. "Brassy" doesn't cover it. This tough and mounding annual is great for tough, hot areas.

Flowering tobacco (*Nicotiana* spp.) comes in several worthy varieties. One favorite is the woodland tobacco (*N. sylvestris*), growing to about 5 feet tall. Its white tubular flowers are fragrant at night. Best of all, woodland tobacco is an aphid trap. The aphids love it and climb on the plant, only to be unable to move off the sticky leaves. Many of the more colorful varieties of nicotiana don't have fragrance but are good summer performers thanks to their pale green, pink, and dark red flowers.

New Guinea impatiens flower in neon bright orchid, pink, and orange colors that enliven the summer landscape. Look for the spectacular flower and foliage colors on plants that take less shade than our easy and more common shade lovers and brighteners, *Impatiens walleriana.*

Love-in-a-mist (*Nigella*), or black cumin, is a reseeding annual that will cover areas with ferny foliage before blooming.

Phormium and **cordyline** have better presence and more color variations than the traditional dracena spike for containers. New Zealand flax (*Phormium* spp.) may winter over in warm areas of Virginia, but it is tender in the northern areas.

Plectranthus spp. are fast growing and perfect for containers, with long branches spilling over the sides of the pot. Look for the versatile yellow-variegated form. A relative of Swedish ivy, some varieties, like silvery *P. argentatus,* grow upright.

Polka-dot plant (*Hypoestes phyllostaschya*) is small with white, red, or pink polka dots on its leaves. Perfect to brighten a shady area.

Salvia is a wonderful family of plants. *Salvia leucantha, S. guaranitica,* and *S. farinacea* are beautiful, tough, and respond well to hot, dry conditions once established. In blues and purples, they add volume and depth to the garden. The pineapple sage, *S. rutilans,* blooms late in bright red, but the leaves are fragrant all summer. Plant it where you will brush by the leaves and release the scent.

Setcresea pallida/Tradescantia pallida 'Purple Heart' has been used as a houseplant for decades. Its deep purple foliage and prostrate habit make it valuable as a ground cover as well. Drought and heat tolerant, it keeps its regal color all season. This plant has come back after winter in protected well-drained locations in northern Virginia and is likely perennial in Eastern Shore and southeastern Virginia.

South African foxglove (*Ceratotheca triloba*) is always in my summer garden. While it looks a bit like foxglove, it flowers from late summer to frost with mauve or white blossoms. Easy to grow from seed that you collected last year.

Spider flower (*Cleome hassleriana*) has a large airy head on 3- to 5-foot-tall stems. It comes in white, pink, and magenta, and, recently, dwarf forms. As the flowers are pollinated, they form long tubular seedpods that appear along the stem, leading to the common name, spider flower. Reseeding is light and seems confined to the magenta forms. This is a great performer in summer, nice in masses, and colorful all season.

Sweet alyssum (*Lobularia maritima*), a member of the mustard family, can tolerate cool weather, so you can get a great start on your low-maintenance garden. Buy a couple of flats of white, lilac, or mixed sweet alyssum and plant them in every open spot. Though this plant looks fragile and moisture loving, it's tough and loves hot and dry locations once established. Its tiny flowers and frothy appearance make it a perfect choice for the garden, diminutive and unobtrusive but perfect to cover the ground.

Mexican sunflower (*Tithonia rotundifolia*) has red orange petals with a bright orange center. Subsequent flowers tend to be lower on the plant than the first flush, leaving spent flowers and seed heads on the top. It requires midseason pruning/touch-up if planted close by.

Zinnia angustifolia is a perfect warm-season, small-flowered, low-growing ground-covering plant for summer. Varieties have white or orange flowers, although the shade of orange is a little muddy and not an easy blender. It spreads horizontally, covering well as it goes. This plant does not require any pruning to look good all summer. It's great to cover areas where daffodil bulbs have gone dormant.

Summer Bulbs

Many summer bulbs are tender and need to be brought inside during the winter, especially caladium, calla lily, dahlia, ginger (*Hedychium coronarium, H. coccineum* and hybrids), gloriosa lily, Peruvian daffodil (*Hymenocallis narcissiflora*), rain lilies (*Zephyranthes* spp.), tuberose (*Polianthes tuberosa*), and tuberous begonia. In warmer portions of Virginia, caladium, canna, and lily of the Nile (*Agapanthus africanus*) can stay in the ground with mulching.

Among my favorite summer bulbs are:

Acidanthera is a fragrant gladiolus reputed to be hardy in northern Virginia, but it is not reliable. It is well worth planting every year for its great fragrance.

Caladiums are grown for great foliage. Green leaves with white or red marbling are lovely in part or deep shade. One of the best plantings I've seen is a half oak barrel with different varieties planted.

Dahlia varieties seem endless. Big cactus flowers and tiny

Storing Dahlia Tubers for Winter

Dig up the plant, remove any soil, and cut off leaves and all but about 2 inches of stem. Let it dry in a sunny location. In a large paper bag or pail, mix eight cups of vermiculite with one cup of sulfur. After cutting back the plants, shake and coat dahlia tubers and central stem material in the mix. Leave it out to dry, letting excess dust fall off, then wrap the whole thing in clear plastic wrap. Use masking tape to identify plant name or color. Store in a frost-free location over the winter.

Plantswoman Karen Rexrode used this new method recommended by a dahlia society to overwinter her dahlias. She was thrilled that "100 percent survived! This method is so much better than storing them in peat moss and takes much less space. All were sprouting in spring."

pompoms in myriad colors are only a few of the choices to make. Several companies have Web sites that will fill you with plant lust in February.

Gladioli are great cut flowers and should be sown in successive plantings for an extended season. Thrips are a major problem; their presence is identified by streaky foliage, flowers, and contorted buds. You will be more successful rotating glads in different planting areas each year.

Flowering gingers (*Hedychium* spp.) are tall and bold in the summer landscape, flowering in pastels. Many varieties are not fragrant. The foliage is not as bold as a canna, and they will like a part-shaded, moist location best. Get a handful of ginger from the supermarket and grow it in a pot. Once the plant is pot bound (after several years), you will be rewarded with an intoxicatingly fragrant white flower in the summer night.

Star-of-Bethlehem (*Ornithogalum nutans*) bulbs are long blooming on 3-foot stems. White star-shaped flowers arrayed in a dome grace any garden. These can be hardy in USDA Zone 7 and warmer.

Tuberoses are a favorite of grower Kathy Gibb. She recommends successive plantings since the flowers are so short-lived. Buying fresh bulbs each year is the key to success. Single or double flowers smell the same. Don't bother to overwinter the bulbs.

Annuals in Containers

Warm weather allows us to enjoy the outdoors from decks, pools, and patios. Plants in containers can brighten and soften these areas. Adding seasonal color to the front door or balcony is welcoming and cheery. Interesting foliage and seasonal flowers add to the enjoyment of container-grown annuals.

Use good quality potting mixes in containers rather than native soil; garden soil contains weed seeds, soil creatures, and bacteria and fungi that can become a problem in containers.

Soilless mix is weed free and not yet colonized by creatures. You can buy potting mixes by the bag or highly compressed bale. Put some in a tub, break it up well, add some time-release fertilizers, moisten, then put it in your container. Once the potting mix is moistened, it will not fall out of the drainage hole. By the way, current research shows that it's not necessary to put gravel in the bottom of a pot. A drainage hole in the bottom is adequate.

When using large containers, you may want to place inverted plastic pots inside the tub to reduce the amount of potting mix needed. Some folks use plastic peanuts covered by a piece of land-scape cloth that keeps pot-ting mix from sifting down into the peanuts. Either approach will work as long as there is enough potting mix to support the plants and the container does not become unstable and top heavy.

Plants in contain-ers have no other resources than the ones you provide. Fertilization is required. Osmocote and other time-release fertilizers are easy to apply, but be aware that they run out of punch after about two months of watering. Renew whenever a plant starts to fade. Liquid fertilizers can be applied at half strength every two weeks or full strength once per month. Liquid fertilization is more work on your part, but results will be good.

Pay attention to watering. You can be fooled by the soil in the pot—the top may be wet, but underneath it is bone dry. Good watering takes time. Set up a rain gauge when you set up the sprinkler. An inch of water in the rain gauge is a good watering session. It's better to water well than to water often. In hot weather some containers will need watering twice a day.

Let's drop some watering myths here. There's no need to worry about watering in the sun; water drops do not burn the leaves. You can water in the evening. Plant roots need air, so don't let them sit in trays of water.

Which annuals work best in containers? Container gardens can include trees and woody plants as well as perennials and annuals. You will want to put plants with similar cultural requirements in the same pot. Shade lovers and sun lovers don't mix well. Strong growers, like 'Margarita' ornamental sweet potatoes, can overrun wispy plants. Plants that need regular food, like hibiscus, will not be happy with desert succulents that love lean soil. Drought-loving red geraniums (*Pelargonium* spp.) and moisture-loving horsetail (*Equisetum* spp.) will be unhappy together.

Growing requirements for a plant don't change just because it's in a container, so excellent drainage, adequate moisture, appropriate food, and sun or shade preferences must still be considered. Winter will still arrive. Perennials and woody plants can be removed from seasonal pots and planted in the ground in early fall. Some large, heavy pots can get through winter without being damaged by freezing conditions, and trees in those pots often survive, but I am reluctant to recommend this practice. Temperatures in winter can be well below freezing, and bitter winds blow above ground, whereas roots carefully protected below the ground only get to 32 degrees.

Container gardening is a great opportunity to try out some plants previously unknown to you. New varieties, tropicals, half-hardy plants, and colorful plants from around the world are available. This year, the Australian plant "kangaroo paws" is popular. Who knows what's next!

Donna's Best Advice: Container Water Gardens

It's fun to grow water plants (like miniature cattail, water chestnut, and lotus) in containers. The plants always look cool and refreshing. Topping off the water in the pot is less burdensome than watering pot after pot of thirsty annuals. Use mosquito dunks of *Bacillus thuringiensis* subsp. *israelensis* to keep the water pest free.

Water gardens are easy to maintain in sunny, hot areas like patios and pools. All of the following plants except the lotus can be grown in soil or water.

Canna spp. include many varieties and are valuable summer tropicals. Often wintering over in Virginia, canna leaves can be green or burgundy or beautifully variegated and mix well in the summer garden. Flowers come in white, yellow, pink, peach, red, pink, and mixed.

Elephant ears are alocasias and colocasias, great tropical foliage plants. Grown in water or soil, these arrowhead-shaped leaves can have exotic black or white variegation and vary in size from modest to huge. Bulbs must winter indoors.

Equisetum spp. exist from dinosaur days. Also called horsetail for its flowering stage, the plants consist of thin, segmented green stems without leaves. The moisture lovers are also called scouring rushes, containing so much silica that you can do fine sanding with them.

Lotuses (*Nelumbo* spp.) have exquisite, huge flat round leaves that repel water, and stand on tall stems like lily pads waiting for a bird to land. The flowers bloom in July and have stunning seed heads. Lotus can take over a pond.

Ruellia brittoniana is a 3-foot-tall upright species petunia with purple blooms.

Annual Vines

Running out of garden ground? Not to worry—go vertical with annuals that will give you a summer full of height and color.

Beans, including purple hyacinth bean (*Dolchios lablab* or *Lablab purpurea*) and scarlet runner bean (*Phaseolus coccineus*), are emblems of summer for me. The orchid flowers of the hyacinth bean and its deep purple pods thrive in hot days. The scarlet runner bean is dainty—red flowers against a lightweight vine. Both are easy to grow. Soak the seeds in water for eight hours before planting to germination. These plants are twiners, so they will need something to climb on. Light wire fencing, string, or lattice will work. They both look good on a twig tepee or other more elaborate garden framework.

Canary vine (*Tropaeolum canariense*) is a member of the nasturtium family. Growing about 12 feet, it sports lovely clean leaves and bright yellow flowers. Grow canary vine on a twiggy tripod so it can wrap its leaves around strong supports. It's very sensitive to frost.

Love-in-a-puff (*Cardiospermum halicacabum*) is considered invasive in Virginia. Take care if you grow this. Named after the heart-shape on the seed, this annual vine forms an airy, fat case to hold its seeds.

Morning glories (*Ipomea* spp.) and their many family members are garden staples. It's hard to be without that bright blue face in the morning. Loving heat and full sun, and given no root disturbance and something to twine on, morning glories thrive. They come in several colors and markings; 'Heavenly Blue' is an old-time beauty. Once morning is taken care of, white moon vines (*I. alba*) bloom during the evening and emit a heady, tropical fragrance. Pollinated by night-flying insects, the plants can be placed near your favorite evening chair or bedroom window. Give both morning glories and moon vines sturdy support; the volume of leaves will surprise you. Both plants are easily grown from seed: Nick the seed coat and soak in water for one day before planting. Don't plant out too early.

Other morning glory relatives include *I. purpurea*, which reseeds and is on the invasive plant list for Virginia. Cypress vine (*I. quamclit*), a little gem, has small, tubular red, white, or pink flowers and ferny green foliage. It reseeds readily in Virginia. *I. lobata* (formerly *Mina lobata*) is stunning with a double array of tubular flowers ranging in color from red to pale yellow. Plants with more than one color can give a garden a lively spirit, and this one can easily reach 12 feet high. A twig or bamboo tripod will provide a great base for this plant.

Still another member of this family, *I. batatas*, contains the food plants valued by much of the world and some highly ornamental vines. Ornamental sweet potatoes have come a long way. 'Margarita', 'Ace of Spades', 'Tricolor', and 'Blackie' are staples of container gardens. New varieties with variegation and finely cut leaves seem to come out each year. Heat-loving sweet potatoes thrive in Virginia summers and can be used as ground covers under shrubs and among lilies and gladioli. Not good climbers, their vines scramble over less vigorous companions and form sheets of foliage as they spill over the sides of large containers.

Mandevilla (*Dipladenia* spp.) is a star of the annual container garden. Bright deep pink or white flowers grace this languorous vine all season. It loves heat but hates drying out. Be sure to give the twining vine something to grow on as well as a biweekly, half-strength dose of water-soluble fertilizer. The glossy leaves add to the tropical look of this useful annual. It is easier to give it the moisture it requires with a big deep pot and a humus-rich mix of potting soil and leaf compost.

Passionflower (*Passiflora caerulea*) is fascinating with its different colors and complicated parts. It's potentially hardy but finicky. Even watering and good drainage are essential. With an application of pine bark mulch, it can survive Virginia winters that don't get below 1 degree Fahrenheit, and it benefits from being planted at a south or east-facing wall. You can also bring passionflower inside during the winter, but don't water it until spring.

Passionflowers come in magenta, red, white, blue, and purple. Most are tropical plants that can be grown as annuals in Virginia. The maypop (*P. incarnata*) exists wild in Virginia. Give passionflowers good support with trellis or tripod so the tendrils can reach out and grab something sturdy. They will benefit from an extra bit of phosphorus and potassium but should not be given much nitrogen fertilizer or excessive leafiness will result at the expense of flowers.

CHAPTER EIGHT

Vegetables and Herbs

No matter what other kinds of gardens you have, or how long you garden, growing vegetables is rewarding and fun. Holding a sun-warmed tomato or snapping a crisp green bean reminds you of the bounty of soil and nature. Whether you grow organically or with limited pesticides, you will taste flavors in your homegrown veggies and herbs that are missing from refrigerated and transported food from the store.

Planting Approaches

Before you start planting those tomatoes and beans, consider these planting ideas.

Rotate plants. Rotating crops in planting beds will help you reduce disease and pest outbreaks. Some pests, like squash bugs, overwinter in the soil. If they hatch and find no curcurbits (pumpkins, cucumbers, squash, melons), they go elsewhere. Tomato diseases like *Verticillium* and *Fusarium* remain in the soil for several years. Planting disease-resistant tomatoes can help, but that limits you to newer varieties. Planting elsewhere is best.

Account for crop height. Tall plants like corn, climbing beans, and big tomato vines can shade other plants. Plant them north of shorter plants.

Elevate beds. Be kind to yourself and build raised beds for your vegetable garden. A raised bed offers many advantages: It is easier on your back, has good drainage, gives you control of soil composition, warms up earlier in spring, eliminates kneeling and squatting, and prevents weeds and grass growing at ground level from infiltrating. It's too tall for rabbits (but just right for deer), can be covered in winter so weed seeds and leaves don't blow in, and you can pick a tomato at eye level!

The thin, upright leaves of the onion family and the open leaf structure of strawberries make them weed collectors. If you can, grow them in raised beds where weed seeds will not fall or collect.

Expect some crop loss. Don't rely on "companion planting" for insect control. Lots of cheerful advisers recommend staging insect-repelling plants near insect favorites to confuse, attract, or repel the marauders. Gardener and garden book author Rita Buchanan calls it "wishful thinking" and reminds us that "insects are good at finding the plants they need in a complex environment." Plant enough for you and the insects.

Try succession planting. This makes the most of the long Virginia growing season. Cool-season plants like lettuce, shallots, peas, arugula, and spinach fade once the temperatures get high. Harvest them and then cut down the plants; replace them with beans, peppers, squash, and tomatoes. As July starts to wane, start planting cool crops again. They will get a warm start but tolerate the cooler weather of October and November.

Add compost to everything. Feed the soil rather than the plant. Since most vegetables are annuals, a top-dressing of a broad-spectrum fertilizer may be helpful to cover all the plant's nutrient needs at the start. As you build better soil, the need for fertilizer will be diminished.

Vegetable Best Bets

There are many vegetables you can grow. When I learned to can, I wanted tomatoes with lots of good flavor, and for that I turned to the heirloom varieties. Peppers and potatoes are easy and enjoyable. Grow what you like to eat and then experiment a little with new things. It's all fun.

Tomatoes are easy to grow. Garden centers offer a broad array of tomato varieties to choose from, and as long as outside

The Warm and Cool of It

Cool-weather crops	Warm-season crops
Arugula	Beans
Beets	Celery
Bok choy (biennial)	Corn
Broccoli	Cucumber
Brussels sprouts	Eggplant
Cabbage	Melon
Carrot	Okra
Cauliflower	Peppers
Chinese cabbage	Potato
Endive	Pumpkin
Garlic	Squash
Kale	Sunflower
Lettuce (sow leaf lettuce	Sweet potato
for fall crops)	Swiss chard
Mustard	Tomato
Onion family	
Parsley (biennial)	
Peas	
Radish	
Spinach	
Turnips	

temperatures are warm, the plants grow well. Some people like to jump the season and plant tomatoes early. Sitting in chilly soil makes tomatoes unhappy, regardless of what you place around them to protect from frost. Wait until temperatures are at least 55 degrees Fahrenheit every night before planting your tomato (and other warm-season) plants.

Heirloom tomatoes have great flavor but are often susceptible to tomato diseases. Newer varieties have resistance built in, but many lack flavor. You might consider growing a few of each.

For fun, be sure to plant the tiny tomatoes: grape, pear, currant, and cherry types. They ripen early and will treat you to a long season of fruit. Unless you are growing for a large family, you won't need more than one plant of each type, because they are surprisingly prolific!

Most tomatoes are vines; few bush types exist, like the 'Patio' tomato. Once the vines get going in summer, they will be rangy and heavy with fruit. Install sturdy stakes at the same time you plant so that you don't damage roots by putting in stakes later. Cages of concrete reinforcing wire make the best supports for vigorous plants with loads of fruit, and the cages can be used for many years.

If you expect rain, harvest any tomatoes that have turned white or have started to color. While drought tolerant, tomatoes can absorb a lot of water in a quick storm, and the ripening fruit will subsequently develop longitudinal cracks.

Blossom end rot can be caused by several conditions, but the most likely is a calcium deficiency. Be sure to add some limestone or gypsum to the soil to avoid the problem.

Peppers are easy to grow. All varieties do well in the heat of June, July, August, and September. Many people plant both the sweet bell peppers and the spicy and hot peppers. A variety called 'Jingle Bells' features small sweet bell peppers in reds and greens, perfect for a small salad! Some varieties are highly ornamental, such as those with variegated purple leaves and tiny hot peppers. Long, chartreuse peppers can be hot or sweet. Be sure to keep the plant tags straight or you might get a taste-bud surprise. Jalapeños and other spicy peppers are good grow-ers and have few pests. The European corn borer can bother peppers, but most other insects leave it alone.

Be careful when harvesting peppers, as the branches are brittle. It's better to cut off the fruit than yank it.

Potatoes are fun to harvest. It's like a treasure hunt to comb through the soil in search of the spuds that form along the roots of the plant. To grow potatoes in containers, start with potatoes that have sprouted in your kitchen, cut them into sections with two eyes/sprouts each, and plant the sections in 2 inches of potting soil at the bottom of a large container with drain holes. As the plants grow, add more soil and leaf compost. Over the season you will notice that some of the plants die off and others keep growing. Once all the plants have started to die, upend the con-tainer and find your potatoes.

Potato scab is a common disease. Dusting the potatoes with garden sulfur at planting time can help them resist infec-tion.

Perennial Vegetables

Most garden vegetables are annuals—but there are exceptions. Fennel, asparagus, and rhubarb are perennial in Virginia. Fennel seeds are delicious, and even the pollen is an ingredient for fancy food chefs! Asparagus and rhubarb will produce over many years. If you buy a pot of rhubarb from a nursery, plant it as is, without removing any potting mix. The roots are extraordinarily brittle when in active growth.

Cucumbers, winter squash, gourds, and pumpkins take up a lot of room in the garden due to their many leaves and long vines. Summer squash (zucchini and yellow squash) doesn't vine, but the plants can still be quite large. Separate male and female flowers form on these plants. The male flowers are on a long stem. On the female flowers, you can see the immature fruit ready to be pollinated. All cucumbers and squashes can be affected by squash vine borers and wilts.

Eggplant. Flea beetles plague young eggplant leaves by puncturing the leaves with tiny holes. If you can cover the young plants with fabric row covers until the plants get to a good size, the problem will have passed. Insects pollinate eggplant, so remove the row cover when the flowers open. Harvest the glossy purple or white fruit when small and tender.

Gardening Resources

Virginia Cooperative Extension offices can provide information on vegetable gardening across the commonwealth. For helpful downloadable fact sheets on fruits and vegetables, visit www.ext.vt.edu/resources and click on Fruits and Vegetables under Educational Programs and Resources. Virginia Tech has experts in nearly every topic.

Books are great resources for the vegetable gardener. Look for *Identifying Diseases of Vegetables* from Pennsylvania State University. Its full-color photographs are extremely helpful when trying to diagnose problems. Eliot Coleman has two practical books on organic gardening. Rosalind Creasy's encyclopedia of edible plants is chock-full of information. Designers and writers Joe Eck and Wayne Winterrowd have a delightful book about their kitchen garden in Vermont, and British author Anna Pavord has a useful book that includes garden designs. Just keep in mind that Virginia is not Britain, Maine, or Vermont. (See chapter 10 for book resources.)

Herbs

Herb gardens are fun and useful. Beverage herbs like hops for beer and lemon balm for tea can give way to culinary herbs like rosemary and dill. Medicinal herbs include peppermint for headaches and arnica for bruises. When you explore the world of herbs, you join the long line of people who have planted and studied these useful plants. You can even grow tropical herbs like patchouli and vetiver for fragrance, adding them to your roses and lavender. The more you learn, the more fun you will have.

Mediterranean Herbs

Greek oregano has great flavor, but most of the oreganos we plant revert to some ancient form with scraggly leaves, poor flavor, and lanky habits. Cousin marjoram acts the same way. Be ruthless. Cut back these plants severely. If they don't taste good to you, rip them out and find better ones. The bees love them all.

Lavender is one of my favorites herbs because both leaves and flowers have great fragrance. Plant lavender on a slope or in a gravel bed. Good varieties include 'Provence' and 'Grosso', also called 'Fat Spike'. Both have long flower stems. Ruthless pruning in late winter keeps the plants growing well. If the plants are allowed to develop extended woody stems, their life is shortened. I resist using lavender as a hedging plant because they can struggle with Virginia winter wet. When one or two plants die in a uniform hedge, the hedge is a long time recovering.

Rosemary is hardy in many parts of Virginia. In northern Virginia it pretends to be hardy and then in March succumbs to winter wet or a mysterious (to me) pathogen. Planting rosemary in a gravel bed can help, as can putting it in sheltered areas with warm walls and excellent drainage. Look for the tasty 'Gorizia'. It grows to 3 feet tall in one season.

Thyme is a plant to experiment with. Buy three or eight different varieties and plant them in your garden. Most will die. Some will winter over but look scraggly and miserable the next spring; you can just rip out the unhappy ones. The thymes that winter well are the best for your garden. Mother-of-thyme is a tiny-leafed, ground-hugging plant that does well in some gardens. French upright thyme is often a survivor. The most successful variety I have found over many gardens is variegated lemon thyme. Wooly thyme needs perfect drainage year-round; even then our humid summers will ruin it. Though upright varieties seem to have the best chance, plantswoman Karen Rexrode thinks the prostrate *T. serpyllum* 'Albus' is best.

Other Delicious Herbs to Grow

Basil is available in many varieties and all should be tasted. Thai basil, spicy miniature globe basil, Genovese basil, and African blue basil are different and delicious. Basil is a warm-weather plant that will not survive a frost. Chop leaves with oil and then freeze the mixture; this preserves the flavor better than drying the leaves.

Coriander is an herb that you love or hate. It's a cool-season grower and quickly goes to seed (still usable) in hot weather.

Dill and fennel are delicious and beneficial to caterpillars. Both will reseed readily. The bronze fennel is beautiful.

Fenugreek is a delicious and unusual herb common in Indian cooking. You can plant the seeds in that dusty herb jar for a tasty green salad herb.

Garlic and shallots are easy to grow and attractive in the perennial garden as well. Plant in fall and harvest at midsummer.

Lemon balm is a fragrant thug, spreading by stolon and seed. Its dried leaves make an excellent tea.

Lemon grass is a delicious tropical grass that grows about 3 feet tall. Harvest from the base of growth, where it is tender.

Parsley is biennial, so you will be planting it repeatedly. According to chefs, the flat-leaf Italian parsley has the best flavor.

Peppermint is a delicious thug. Black peppermint has the strongest flavor. Contain this plant or it will be everywhere, swamping other plants quickly. Rub the leaves on your face as a gnat repellent. Make your own mint ice cream.

Be careful—herb growing is addictive!

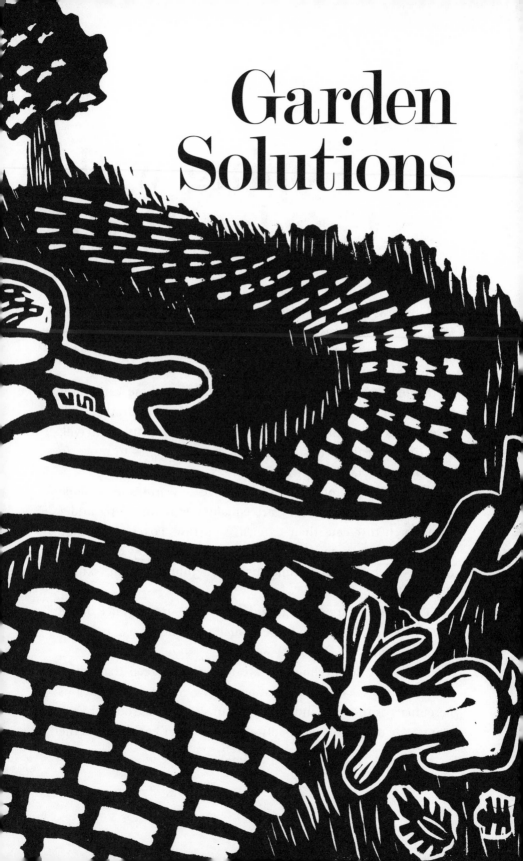

Garden
Solutions

Coping with Garden Pests

Garden pests come in many forms. They can be your furry friends—dogs and cats—or wild critters like skunks, groundhogs, or deer. They can be tiny insects that strip the leaves off your plants. There are ways to handle these pests.

Moles. People complain about moles, but these carnivores don't eat plants. They eat Japanese beetle grubs and other soil-dwelling insects. Using milky spore disease on your lawn will, over time, kill the grubs and encourage your moles to move to someone else's lawn.

Groundhogs (or woodchucks) love a warm sunny slope along the highway, but they are equally happy tunneling under your porch to create their extensive burrow. Foxes (and some dogs) eradicate them. These herbivores forage only during the day. If you have a nighttime marauder, think raccoon, skunk, deer, rabbit, or opossum.

Chipmunks are darling unless they take up residence in the stone wall bordering your perennial bed and snack on your favorite plants.

Voles are not darling and are more widespread than chipmunks. They create tunnels under snow, eating your delicious perennials as they go, and use mole runs to eat the roots of your plants. I've had plants wilt badly a few days after I put them in the ground. I touch the plant and the top comes away in my hands—no roots at all! That's vole damage.

My remedy for groundhogs, chipmunks, and voles is to place a clump of urine-soaked kitty litter in their entrance hole. They don't know how big the cat is, and thus they'll go elsewhere. This approach may require some persistence. Cats can be slightly effective if they are hunters, but voles multiply like . . .

Rabbits eat seedlings, new plants, bark on fruit trees, and spring growth of ornamental grasses. Having tried all the standard remedies, I have found that nothing works except foxes and the occasional cat. Make it harder for rabbits. Put wire or plastic guards at the base of fruit trees. Look inside that big clump of ornamental grass for a nest and add some used kitty litter. Fence off young seedlings.

Deer may taste but will not eat boxwood and pieris. Other than those two plants, everything else appears on their menu at times. They will eat sharp holly leaves and prickly juniper. They routinely eat yew (*Taxus*), which is toxic to most animals. My best advice is that you observe the normal deer route and don't plant anything near that route that encourages them to come closer to your garden. No daylilies, no hosta, no roses. Deer notice and taste anything new in the environment. They may even taste your new boxwood. If there is nothing delicious, they will move on and find other sources of food, like your neighbor's daylilies.

Domestic cats can cause serious damage to young trees when they use them as scratching posts. Wrapping the trunks with Vetrap annoys cats sufficiently to make them go scratch on some of the lumber used in your raised beds. Used to cover bandages on pets and horses, Vetrap is made of rubber latex and has air pores so the bark doesn't get moist underneath. It feels slightly tacky to the touch and that's why the cats don't like it. Available in a wide range of colors, it loses its elasticity after about a year, when it starts to droop rather than girdle the tree. Remove the wrap or, if you think the cat will persist, rewrap the trunk gently for another year and create a scratching post for the cat elsewhere.

Dogs are great garden companions, but their urine can burn growing plants. If you can, place obstacles around your vulnerable plants so that male dogs urinate on the obstacle—rock, log, statue, or gazing ball—rather than the plant. If you witness the event, reduce the damage by applying fresh water to thoroughly dilute the urine. You can track your female dog by the yellowed grass spots. Again, try to dilute. In low doses, urea (or urine) is a form of nitrogen. The level of concentration is key.

Insects—Friends or Foes?

The world is complicated. In some cases insects are beneficial to the gardener's purposes because they eat unwanted pests voraciously. Sometimes those same insects are damaging: For instance, the generally beneficial praying mantis unfortunately also eats our flower-pollinating bees as well as damaging aphids and other pesky critters. People dislike and fear wasps, yet wasps eat many caterpillars. Tent caterpillars are reviled, but many of our songbirds love to eat them.

The following insects should be considered beneficial (to us gardeners) in most instances:

Fireflies are predators in their larval stage, feeding on slugs and snails.

Ladybugs and **lacewings** are commonly known beneficial insects.

Praying mantis is a great predator, although it will eat bees critical for pollination as well as aphid pests. Their tan, plastic-looking egg cases will be visible at summer's end and may be accidentally discarded when you prune woody plants in winter. These insects are fascinating predators, turning their heads to watch prey.

Spiders catch and devour many insect pests. The yellow and black argiope is a classic garden spider with colorful markings and a signature web. In the center of the web is a white zigzag designed to prevent birds from flying through and destroying it. Harvestman spiders, or daddy longlegs, are common in most gardens. They feed on small insects like aphids.

Wasps are major predators of worms and caterpillars. Unless they are nesting in an area that is dangerous to you, leave them alone. White-faced wasps create a big, gray paper nest in shrubs and trees. They are not as aggressive as the brown wasps that create mud-tube nests on almost any vertical surface.

Wheel bugs, also called assassin bugs, are large insects with a long, curved beak where their nose should be. Their eggs are often found on smooth-barked trees in a flat-topped, raised pentagon shape of minute gray black eggs. Red or green when they hatch, the nymphs are smaller versions of the gray adults. They eat Japanese and other beetles, leafhoppers, spittlebugs, and insect eggs. They can bite if handled.

Most of the good insect predators listed above will thrive in your garden as long as you do not apply pesticides. Growing nectar plants like dill, fennel, and asters with your other plants will help support a diverse and bountiful array of insects. Predatory insects and nematodes are commercially available. Some providers can be contacted at these Web sites: www.rincon vitova.com, www.arbico-organics.com, and www.dirtworks.com.

The following insects are traditionally considered annoying pests. But they have good qualities, so please use pesticides sparingly—if at all.

Bagworms affect spruces, Leyland cypress, and arborvitae, Virginia red cedar, and other juniper species. It takes several years for populations to build up large enough to defoliate and kill the tree. Hiding in a bag made of leaves, the pest is protected, and its eggs overwinter in the bags. Handpick, squish, and destroy the bags. Pheromone traps can be used in August to trap males before they mate with females. You can also apply *Bacillus thuringiensis* var. *kurstaki*. These bacteria produce crystal toxins that poison and kill the bagworm caterpillar as it feeds.

Black blister beetles travel in large groups and can defoliate clematis, grape, and Japanese anemones. Don't touch them with bare hands, and don't kill them. Use a broom in a sweeping motion to move the group of beetles along. They are great predators of grasshopper eggs, which is good, because grasshopper invasions can strip your plants bare.

Black vine weevil grubs feed on roots of strawberry, primrose, tiarella, heuchera, and bramble fruit plants. They are about ⅛ inch long and look like a white grub. Remove soil from nursery-purchased plants and destroy the grubs, or obtain parasitic nematodes to treat the soil.

Iris borers are a major pest of bearded or German irises. In July dig up weak or watery-looking irises, cut back the leaves to 3 or 4 inches tall, and check the rhizomes. Feel for soft, squishy areas and a bad odor. Soft-rot bacteria often follow the borer's trail into the rhizome. Cut away soft, brown areas to firm, white tissue. Find the pink borer with the brown head and kill it. To kill any remaining soft-rot bacteria, soak the cleaned-up rhizome in a bucket with water and 10 percent chlorine bleach for ten minutes. Allow the rhizome to dry in the sun, then dust it with garden sulfur. Replant the rhizome at soil level so the sun hits it.

Japanese beetles attack roses, grapes, crab apples, and a few other plants. The beetles appear in northern Virginia around mid-June for six weeks, earlier in more southern areas of the state. Cut off rose flowers, give the plants some food, and knock any beetles into a pail of soapy water. They don't swim. Without succulent, fragrant, and delicious rose flowers to nibble on, the beetles often head elsewhere. Don't suffer over the damage they do. If you must use those pheromone bags that attract more beetles than they kill, place them as far away from your flowers as possible.

Japanese beetles like to lay their eggs in short grass. Your lawn is perfect. The eggs become ground-dwelling grubs that hatch from the lawn and eat grass roots. In July let your grass grow a bit longer—3 or 4 inches is usually enough—so that the beetles will go to your neighbor's lawn to lay eggs. Drought reduces the next generation of beetles, because eggs laid on the grass dry out. So don't be too eager to water your dry brown lawn in later July and August—it will green up by itself in the fall with fewer Japanese beetles. Applying milky spore disease is a long-term control method that takes about five years to be very effective. Milky spore attacks the grub stage of the beetle and, once established, milky spore will remain in the soil for years. Get your neighbors to apply milky spore as well or it's a waste of time and money: The beetles will simply fly over to your yard.

Scarlet lily beetles voraciously feed on lilies, eating the leaves. These insect pests have been moving south from the northeastern United States. The larvae look like drippy, slimy brown poop on the underside of the leaf. Remove the whole leaf because it's too disgusting to touch the larvae and destroy them. Report the beetle's presence to the Virginia Cooperative Extension office near you so that its progress from New England can be tracked. The insecticides Malathion, in a foliar spray, or Sevin, either as a spray or dust, can be used to kill this pest. Follow label instructions carefully. Spray or dust in the evening when bees go home, as they are sensitive to Sevin and we need them to pollinate fruits and vegetable crops.

Slugs eat decomposing matter, including pet poop. Both slugs and snails can leave ragged holes in the leaves of your hosta, lettuce, and other leafy plants. Protect specific plants with strips of copper flashing around beds or pots. While older formulations of poisons were toxic to pets as well the slugs, new safer formulas with iron phosphate attract and kill the slugs.

Squash bug, squash vine borer, flea beetle, and potato bug are problem insects in vegetable gardens. Cover plants with light sheets of spun polyester (sold under the brand name Reemay) to protect your plants. Remove the fabric briefly so that insects can pollinate squash and eggplant flowers. You can also hand-pollinate squash and eggplant if necessary, although there's no need to pollinate potato plants. Slit the stem of a squash vine to kill the vine borer. Cover the slit with soil so that the vine can heal.

Tent caterpillars. On a sunny day in winter, look at the branches of cherry, apple, and crab apple trees in your yard. Toward the outside end of a branch you may see a short, shiny, black-plastic-looking swelling around the branch. This is the egg case of the tent caterpillar. It's brittle in winter and you can easily snap it off. Drop it on the ground to be eaten by scavenging mice, voles, or other critters.

These furry caterpillars are native and prefer the wild black cherries that fill our woodlands. While they will defoliate a wild cherry, the trees are able to recover readily. Birds like cuckoos, warblers, mockingbirds, white-breasted nuthatches, Baltimore orioles, blue jays, and chickadees eat the caterpillars. The tent material provides nesting material for many birds.

If you snap off the egg cases in winter, it will save you from trying to get the nests out of your ornamental or fruiting cherry. By the time the forsythia blooms, the egg case has become tan and gummy. When you start to see the small tents being woven, take a stick or a broom handle with a nail or cup hook in the end. Wind up the tent and the caterpillars. Don't use a propane torch or other fire source. Your tree can catch on fire . . . a bigger problem than the munching caterpillars. Sprays are often ineffective because the tent is protective. It continues to expand with new sections as the interior sections fill with poop and debris. Keep destroying the nests in your ornamental trees, and next winter look for the egg cases.

Tomato and tobacco hornworms are caterpillars of narrow-wing sphinx moths. They can defoliate your tomato plants over the weekend. They are the same color as your plant and are hard to see. Look for the poop trail. If you see that the hornworm has what looks like rice grains on its back, leave it alone. The "rice" are cocoons spun by larvae of parasitic wasps, tiny beneficial insects that will feed on the hornworm.

Yellow jackets are related to wasps and eat caterpillars and flies. They create a paper nest in the ground and can be a problem. A lawn mower running over the entrance hole or a gardener weeding nearby the nest can enrage them, especially in fall, causing them to attack you, stinging repeatedly and in large numbers.

This has happened to several of us. The first attackers mark you with scent and dozens more follow. They can sting through your clothes. Running water from a hose over my head saved me. Twenty minutes later I returned and members of the hive were still ferociously attacking my weed bucket. Wasp sprays applied in the early evening can kill them if necessary. These sprays also kill vegetation, so use care.

Integrated Pest Management

Integrated pest management (IPM) is a strategy to reduce the use and cost of pesticides while preventing major insect damage to crops. For the home gardener, the idea behind IPM is this: Rather than use the most toxic, broad-spectrum pesticide to kill your insect neighbors, you carefully target the specific pest outbreak when it exceeds a threshold level. In other words, you don't make preemptive strikes against insects that may not ever cause a serious problem.

Under the principles of IPM, you can often control pests by modifying your gardening approach first. For instance, plants that are stressed by too dry or wet locations, poor planting practices, excessive fertilization, or too much sun or shade will be targets for major insect infestations. Put the right plant in the right place, and feed the soil, and you can minimize insect damage.

Remember that most plants growing well in the landscape can easily tolerate some insect activity. Early-flowering honeysuckle (like the native *Lonicera sempervirens*) and roses can suffer from aphids during their early spring bloom period, although the aphids generally find other things to eat after spring. At the same time, aphids provide an important food source for young predatory beneficial insects. Learn to tolerate some insects.

Consider a couple of things about pests.

IPM and the Volterra principle. Be careful when trying to control pests you don't inadvertently destroy the pests' natural predators and thus make the pest problem worse—a situation known as the Volterra principle. Predators like wolves and foxes and praying mantis are born once per year and have a long period of development. In contrast, their prey—mice, rabbits, aphids—breed frequently and hatch larger numbers of offspring. When someone uses a broad-spectrum pesticide or poison to kill the prey, the predators are killed as well. The surviving prey recover rapidly and multiply again that same year, but the predators take another year to rebound. So in effect, the pests you tried to kill with the poison come back without their natural predators, and you end up with more pests rather than fewer.

In the same vein, when you fence out the deer, the foxes are kept out too. Foxes keep rabbits at modest levels. The rabbit population explodes without a predator.

IPM and phenology. There are seasonal explosions of insects, like aphids, that affect the new growth on plants. When using a least toxic (IPM) approach, the idea is to apply insect control when the bugs are active. Look for evidence of the pest, such as boxwood psyllid, around the time of year when they are likely to appear. In northern Virginia the psyllid eggs hatch around tax day, and you begin to see damage in late April and early May. Psyllids feast inside new boxwood growth, so if you prune off and destroy the new tips in May, you can reduce the psyllid population. No spraying is required. And since psyllids are enclosed within the leaves, spraying is generally useless anyway.

You can roughly predict when insects will become active through phenology, the study of climactic effects on the development of plants and animals. Flowering plants and insects both respond to accumulating heat during the growing season. You can track the emergence of flowers and the hatching of insects from year to year. Growing degree day (GDD) statistics are derived from the difference of the average daily temperatures to the baseline of 50 degrees Fahrenheit.

$$\frac{\text{Maximum temperature} + \text{minimum temperature}}{2} - \text{base temperature} = \text{GDD}$$

So if the temperature today is 47 degrees in the morning and 73 degrees in late afternoon:

$$47 + 73 = \frac{120}{2} = 60 - 50 \text{ (base temperature)} = 10 \text{ GDD}$$

The GDD number starts at the beginning of the growing season and accumulates each day. In other words, you take today's 10 GDD number and add that to the GDD numbers for yesterday and last week and so on. Tomorrow you will do the same. Keep a cumulative total. If you track these numbers, you will learn that lilac borers emerge at about 275 to 500 GDD, when the lilac has about finished its bloom. More information about GDD and insect pests can be found at the Chesterfield County Cooperative Extension Web site (http://chesterfield.gov/HumanServices/Extensionservices/gdd.asp). Good information on both phenology and GDD exist on the Internet. Virginia Tech, Cornell, and Ohio State Universities do extensive research in this area.

Once you are able to identify the blooming plants that correlate to the emergence of your common insect pests, you can be alert to controlling higher than normal outbreaks. This system is especially useful with vegetable gardens. Take the case of flea beetles. They eat tiny holes in the leaves of eggplant seedlings, and they emerge at about 150 to 200 GDD—that is, at the same time redbuds are coming into early bloom and the amelanchiers are in full bloom. Because you know when the flea beetles will emerge, you can cover young eggplants with Reemay fabric in early spring to help prevent flea beetle damage; then you uncover the eggplants later in the season when they flower for pollination.

All in all, the IPM approach strives to minimize unintended consequences. Instead of automatically reaching for the big insecticide guns, you start by adjusting your approach to gardening. Good cultural conditions with balanced nutrition and healthy soils will make the most difference in controlling pests in the garden.

CHAPTER TEN

Resources for the Virginia Gardener

Experience is the best teacher, but other resources can help round out your growth as a gardener. Sharing your experience with fellow green thumbs is best. Here are some other resources.

Cooperative Extension Programs

The Virginia Cooperative Extension offices form a superb network of resources for any gardener. Each county office can put you in touch with experts, Virginia Cooperative Extension master gardeners, and an array of helpful publications. Headquartered at Virginia Tech in Blacksburg, the Cooperative Extension network includes 107 county extension offices and several research stations where additional information is available. Find out more at www.ext.vt.edu.

Here are some of the Agricultural Research and Extension Centers (AREC) and their research specialties.

Alson H. Smith Jr. AREC (Winchester): fruit trees

Eastern Shore AREC: vegetables and field crops

Eastern Virginia AREC: plant breeding

Hampton Roads AREC: environmental horticulture industry, landscape, and urban trees

Middleburg AREC: equine and pastures
Northern Piedmont AREC: livestock production and forages
Reynolds Homestead AREC: forest biology
Shenandoah Valley AREC: livestock production and forages
Southern Piedmont AREC: sustainable crops
Southwest Virginia AREC: sheep, blueberries, pumpkins, Christmas trees
Southwest Virginia AqAREC: aquaculture and alternative horticulture
Tidewater AREC: vegetables, swine, and small grains
Virginia Seafood AREC: seafood and aquaculture

Master Gardener Program

The Virginia Master Gardener Program is not available at all offices, but it's worth your time to seek out the closest location where master gardener training and volunteer activities are centered. Training in research-based horticultural information is free and extensive, but those in the training program must purchase an excellent resource notebook for about $100. A volunteer commitment is required as part of the training. Some of the activities that volunteers work on include demonstration gardens, answer desk coverage, plant and weed identification at garden fairs, and other public events and efforts. Benefits of the master gardener program, besides the gardening education, include fellowship with other folks sharing your interests and delights. Visit www.hort.vt.edu/master gardener for details. Once you become a master gardener, you might consider joining the Virginia Master Gardener Association (www.vmga.net), a group dedicated to continuing education and information and a wonderful resource in itself.

Soil Testing

Soil and pathogen testing is done through the Cooperative Extension offices in Blacksburg. Visit the Web site at www.ext.vt.edu. Information about contacting your county office is available there.

Plant Societies

Select a plant you love and join its plant society. Membership will often include newsletters from other people who love those plants. Attend their meetings. Don't say anything if you wish; just listen to members speak about what they know and why they admire these plants. Learn from them. Share their passion. And if you join the Magnolia Society International, buy some seeds and grow your own magnolias. If you find you love another plant more, switch societies. Here are just a few to consider:

American Boxwood Society: www.boxwoodsociety.org
American Clematis Society: http://clematis.org
American Conifer Society: www.conifersociety.org
American Hosta Society: www.hosta.org
American Peony Society: www.americanpeonysociety.org
Magnolia Society International: www.magnoliasociety.org
National Chrysanthemum Society: www.mums.org
Virginia Native Plant Society: www.vnps.org

Public and Private Gardens

Visiting public and private gardens will enrich and expand your point of view. Some gardens seem ordinary, while others are exquisite in execution and awe inspiring. Each visit builds your knowledge and idea toolbox. You learn from them all, even when the style or design is very different from yours. Unusual plant combinations, interesting use of a common plant, design solutions for slopes or walkways, approaches to shade or bright sun, rose varieties that do well in Virginia, and development of focal points are among many features that inspire, refresh, and enlighten. Some ideas will be worth stealing. I got the idea to use deer-repelling common sage as a ground cover when visiting a garden.

When you find a wonderful garden, visit at different times of the year in different years. Take fellow gardeners along. See how the garden staffers handle a wet area. What do they use as ground covers? What plants appear in their best container plantings? What new plants are they using well? What have they changed this year? Why? Learn from them. Copy them.

The Garden Club of Virginia (www.gcvirginia.org) sponsors annual statewide tours of private gardens in April, and many local garden clubs hold summer tours. Sometimes private gardens are opened for private tours you can join. And there are the gardens of your friends.

A bit about garden etiquette. Ask permission before taking pictures. Ask questions and take notes if you can. Memory is fleeting, especially after looking at an entire garden. You may not remember the name of that exquisite rose. No picking flowers or grabbing seeds, please. Wear comfortable, stable shoes.

Below are some favorite gardens open to the public. Some request admission, but many are free.

Brent and Becky's Bulbs and Gardens, 7900 Daffodil Lane, Gloucester; (877) 661-2852; www.brentandbeckysbulbs .com. Though this garden is all about bulbs, it has so many varieties that it is charming and educational. Look for an opportunity to tour the fields in March and April for an eye-opening daffodil education. Open for tours only.

Colonial Williamsburg, Williamsburg; (800) 447-8679; www.history.org. This historic site is a charming example of garden design where human scale, functionality, and boxwood hedging combine.

Dumbarton Oaks, R and Thirty-first Streets, NW (garden entrance), Washington, D.C.; (202) 339-6401; www.doaks.org. The gardens are the work of twentieth-century landscape designer Beatrix Farrand. Those interested in design elegance should not miss this site.

Gari Melcher Home and Studio, 224 Washington Street, Fredericksburg; (540) 654-1015; www.garimelchers.org. A lovely rose garden grows here.

Glen Burnie Historic Home and Gardens, 901 Amherst Street, Winchester; (540) 662-1473; www.shenandoahmuseum .org. Glen Burnie now also hosts the Museum of the Shenandoah Valley. The gardens are interesting and include many hedged garden rooms; a crab apple walkway; several follies; rose, cutting, and vegetable gardens; and remarkable fish ponds. The late Lee Taylor spent more than thirty years designing and refining this garden. Well worth a trip.

Green Spring Gardens Park, 4603 Green Spring Road, Alexandria; (703) 642-5173; www.greenspring.org. This is one of the premier public gardens in Virginia. Designed to be approachable, practical, and useful to the home gardener, its lush plantings of annuals, fruit trees, ornamental grasses, and native perennials provide beauty and education.

Hampton Roads Arboretum and Display Garden, Virginia Tech Agricultural Research and Extension Center, 1444 Diamond Springs Road, Virginia Beach; (757) 363-3900. A visit here is especially useful to bay and wetland-area gardeners, as displays demonstrate buffer zone and bayscaping plantings. There is a small arboretum and an official trial and All-America Display Garden of annuals each summer.

Hillwood Museum and Gardens, 4155 Linnean Avenue, NW, Washington, D.C.; (202) 686-5807; www.hillwoodmuseum .org. An exquisite garden at the former home of Marjorie Merriweather Post.

Lewis Ginter Botanical Garden, 1800 Lakeside Avenue, Richmond; (804) 262-9887; www.lewisginter.org. Daylily lovers will especially enjoy the plantings at this garden. Well-labeled trees and plantings help gardeners identify plants. Enjoy the new conservatory.

Meadowlark Botanical Gardens Regional Park, 9750 Meadowlark Gardens Court (off Beulah Road), Vienna; (703) 255-3631; www.nvrpa.org/meadowlark.html. This lovely garden is best visited in late summer, when the annual combinations are robust and exquisite.

Monticello, 931 Thomas Jefferson Parkway (5 miles from Charlottesville); (434) 984-9822; www.monticello.org. The home of Thomas Jefferson, great gardener and plantsman, is one of the jewels of America. Restoration has brought it back to life.

Montpelier, 11407 Constitution Highway, Montpelier Station; (540) 672-2728; www.montpelier.org. This lovely home of President James Madison has been undergoing a restoration that removed changes installed by the DuPonts.

Mount Vernon Estate and Gardens, George Washington Parkway, Mount Vernon; (703) 780-2000; www.mountvernon.org. The home of George Washington is fascinating and well restored. Boxwood and practical gardens, with beautiful old trees, grace this distinctive site.

Norfolk Botanical Garden, 6700 Azalea Garden Road, Norfolk; (757) 441-5830; www.norfolkbotanicalgarden.org. Highlights include a wonderful rose garden, an excellent butterfly garden, innovative plantings of seasonal annuals, and great trees, especially crape myrtles.

Oatlands Plantation, 20850 Oatlands Plantation Lane, Leesburg; (703) 777-3174; www.oatlands.org. Visit here to see a walled garden with old boxwood, a very old English oak, a newly restored kitchen garden, a cutting garden, and distinctive seasonal plantings.

Smithsonian Gardens, Washington, D.C.; www.si.gov. Distinctive and well-cared-for gardens are found in the midst of the big museums of the Mall:

- Butterfly Garden (Natural History Museum at Ninth Street). This is a delight for all ages.
- Enid Haupt Garden (Smithsonian Castle/Independence Avenue). A garden with a charming Victorian flair.
- Heirloom Garden (American History Museum). A treat and an education at the same time.
- Katherine Dulin Folger Rose Garden (Arts & Industries Building/Mall). A summer show-off.

- Mary Livingston Ripley Garden (Arts & Industries Building/ Hirshhorn Museum). An excellent example of a lovely and sophisticated four-season garden with great diversity of interesting plants fitted into a narrow space between buildings. Well-labeled.
- Native Plants Garden (American Indian Museum). This garden was designed by Native Americans to showcase the plants and landscape of four local habitats indigenous to the region.

The State Arboretum of Virginia, Blandy Experimental Farm/Orland E. White Arboretum, 400 Blandy Farm Lane (Route 50), Boyce; (540) 837-1758; www.virginia.edu/blandy. The arboretum includes many specimen trees grown to maturity, the world's most extensive collection of boxwood, several native plant areas, a ginkgo grove, and a charming herb garden.

U.S. Botanic Garden, 245 First Street, SW, Washington, D.C.; (202) 225-8333; www.usbg.gov. In a recently renovated building, you'll find well-developed displays of plants from different climates.

U.S. National Arboretum, 3501 New York Avenue, NE, Washington, D.C.; (202) 245-2726; www.usna.usda.gov. This is a great resource for gardeners. The herb garden is extensive, and the old rose display is breathtaking in May. Bonsai, camellias, well-grown trees, a spring display of azaleas, and a summer display of water lilies are among the year-round attractions.

Virginia Zoological Park, 3500 Granby Street, Norfolk; (757) 441-2374; www.virginiazoo.org. This site's several interesting horticultural displays include mature monkey puzzle trees.

Books

Among the most useful tools for Virginia gardeners is the book by Dr. Bonnie Lee Appleton, *The New York/Mid-Atlantic Gardener's Book of Lists.* Virginia experts participated in the development of the listings for every gardening situation and style. Bonnie

Appleton is one of the most knowledgeable garden people on the planet. Don't miss this book.

In most cases, the authors listed below have written several inspiring and informative books. I've listed a fraction of their work here; you will benefit from reading the rest.

Adkins, L. M., Joe Cook, and Monica Cook. *Wildflowers of the Appalachian Trail*. Birmingham, AL: Menasha Ridge, 2006.

Appleton, Bonnie Lee, and L. T. Chaplin. *The New York/Mid-Atlantic Gardener's Book of Lists*. Dallas: Taylor Trade, 2001.

Armitage, Allan. *Armitage's Garden Perennials*. Portland, OR: Timber Press, 2000.

Brooklyn Botanic Garden. *Soils*. Brooklyn, NY: Brooklyn Botanic Garden, 1990.

Buchanan, Rita. *A Weaver's Garden*. Loveland, CO: Interweave Press, 1987.

Burrel, C. Colston. *Perennial Combinations*. Emmaus, PA: Rodale Press, 1999.

Cloyd, R. A., P. L. Nixon, and N. R. Pataky. *IPM for Gardeners*. Portland, OR: Timber Press, 2004.

Coleman, Eliot. *Four-Season Harvest*. White River Junction, VT: Chelsea Green, 1999.

———. *The New Organic Grower*. Chelsea, VT: Chelsea Green, 1989.

Creasy, Rosalind. *The Gardener's Handbook of Edible Plants*. San Francisco: Sierra Club Books, 1986.

Damrosch, Barbara. *The Garden Primer*. New York: Workman, 1988.

Darke, Rick. 2002. *The American Woodland Garden*. Portland, OR: Timber Press, 2002.

———. *The Encyclopedia of Grasses for Livable Landscapes*. Portland, OR: Timber Press, 2007.

Dirr, Michael. *Manual of Woody Landscape Plants*. Champaign, IL: Stipes, 1998.

DiSabato-Aust, Tracy. *The Well-Tended Perennial Garden*. Portland, OR: Timber Press, 1998.

Druse, Ken. *The Natural Habitat Garden*. Portland, OR: Timber Press, 2004.

Eck, Joe, and Wayne Winterrowd. *Living Seasonally*. New York: Henry Holt, 1999.

Eddison, Sydney. *The Gardener's Palette*. New York: Contemporary Press, 2003.

Ellis, Barbara W. *Covering Ground*. North Adams, MA: Storey, 2007.

Gillman, Jeff. *The Truth about Garden Remedies*. Portland, OR: Timber Press, 2006.

Harper, Pam. *Time-Tested Perennials*. Portland, OR: Timber Press, 2000.

Hayward, Gordon. *Garden Paths*. Charlotte, VT: Camden House, 1993.

Heath, Brent, and Becky Heath. *Daffodils for North American Gardens*. Albany, TX: Bright Sky Press, 2001.

———. *Tulips for North American Gardens*. Albany, TX: Bright Sky Press, 2001.

Jeavons, John. *How to Grow More Vegetables*. Berkeley: Ten Speed Press, 1991.

Joyce, David. *Pruning and Training Plants*. Buffalo, NY: Firefly Books, 2002.

Lacy, Allen. *The Inviting Garden*. New York: Henry Holt, 1998.

Loewer, Peter. 1992. *Tough Plants for Tough Places*. Emmaus, PA: Rodale Press, 1992.

Male, Carolyn. *100 Heirloom Tomatoes for the American Garden*. New York: Workman, 1999.

Ogren, Thomas L. *Allergy-Free Gardening*. Berkeley: Ten Speed Press, 2000.

Pirone, P. P., J. R. Hartman, M. A. Sall, and T. P. Pirone. *Tree Maintenance*. New York: Oxford University Press, 1988.

Rochester, Margot. *Earthly Delights*. Lanham, MD: Taylor Trade, 2004.

Schenk, George. *The Complete Shade Gardener*. Portland, OR: Timber Press, 2002.

Shigo, Alex L. *A New Tree Biology*. Durham, NH: Shigo and Trees, 1989.

Springer, Lauren. *The Undaunted Garden*. Golden, CO: Fulcrum, 1994.

Tanner, Ogden. *Living Fences*. Shelburne, VT: Chapters, 1995.

Tolley, Emelie and C. Mead. *Herbs*. New York: Clarkson Potter, 1985.

Tripp, Kim, and J. C. Raulston. *The Year in Trees*. Portland, OR: Timber Press, 2002.

Turnbull, Cass. *Cass Turnbull's Guide to Pruning*. Seattle: Sasquatch Books, 2004.

Verey, Rosemary. *The Garden in Winter*. Boston: Little, Brown, 1988.

Useful Web Sites

www.ahs.org. American Horticultural Society

www.ashdownroses.com. Roses via mail order

www.brentandbeckysbulbs.com. Bulbs via mail order

www.chambleeroses.com. Roses via mail order

www.clematisnursery.com. Clematis via mail order

www.cnr.vt.edu/dendro/dendrology/idit.htm. Helps you identify trees

www.dwfinegardening.com. Donna Williamson's Web site

www.ediblelandscaping.com. Virginia nursery for fruit trees, etc.

www.ext.vt.edu/pubs. Publications of the Cooperative Extension Offices at Virginia Tech

www.extension.iastate.edu/pages/hancock/hort/educ/GBRoses .html. Buck roses

www.gcvirginia.org. Garden Clubs of Virginia

www.greergardens.com. Plants via mail order

www.kitchengardeners.org. Vegetable growing newsletter

www.nationalcapitaldahlia.org. Dahlia society

www.npn.uwm.edu. National Phenology Network

www.oldhousegardens.com. Bulbs via mail order

www.plantdelights.com. Mail order plants

www.ppdl.purdue.edu/ppdl. Plant and pest diagnostic laboratory

www.rareplants.com. Specialty plants mail order

www.raupplab.umd.edu. Dr. Raupp's insect lab Web site

www.RickDarke.com. Author Rick Darke's Web site

www.smallfarms.cornell.edu. Online publications from Cornell

www.soils.usda.gov/survey. Soil surveys by county and state

www.soiltest.vt.edu/soiltest.html. Virginia Tech soil testing

www.theplantlady.net. Karen Rexrode's articles and photos

www.thepruningschool.com. Peter Deahl's pruning information

www.treesplease.com. Ed Milhous, consulting arborist

www.usna.usda.gov. U.S. National Arboretum

www.virginiaplaces.org/regions/physio.html. Virginia physio-graphic regions

Glossary

Abscission. The separation and shedding of a leaf from a self-healing scar.

Allelopathy. The influence of one plant upon another through chemical interaction.

Annual. A plant that goes from seed to maturity and death in one season.

Auxin. A chemical that affects cell and plant growth, especially in trees.

Bark. Dead outer tissue of woody plants.

Biennial. A plant that has only leafy growth in the first year, then flowers, produces seed, and dies in the second year.

Bolting. Premature flowering and seed formation in cool-season plants.

Branch collar. A slightly swollen area at the base of the branch of a tree.

Bulb. A modified underground stem, including corms, rhizomes, tubers, etc.

Conifer. A plant that grows cones.

Crown. In perennial plants, a central point at ground level where new growth emerges in spring. In trees, the upper leafy area of the tree.

Cultivar. A cultivated variety of a plant.

Deciduous. A plant that looses its leaves during dormancy.

Dormant. In an inactive, nongrowing state, as in winter.

Dwarf. A smaller than normal variety; it may mean a 10-foot-tall or a 40-foot-tall rather than a 60-foot-tall tree.

Established. Growing on its own in the landscape.

Evergreen. A plant with green or living foliage throughout the year.

Fastigate. Growing upright naturally, with branching and twigs close together.

Fertile. Capable of producing fruit and seed.

Genus. A group of plants sharing fundamental characteristics but differing in small ways.

Ground cover. A plant that grows densely and can spread or fill in.

Habit. How a plant characteristically grows.

Habitat. The location and surroundings where a plant grows.

Hardening-off. Conditioning to withstand environmental stress, like winter.

Hardy. A plant that can survive winter.

Heaving. Upward movement caused by freeze/thaw cycles.

Herbaceous. A plant with no woody plant stems above ground.

Inflorescence. Flowering portion of a plant.

Lateral. Borne on the sides, as in branches or flower buds.

Leaf. The organ of photosynthesis.

Margin. The edge of a leaf.

Mulch. Material placed on soil to prevent erosion or weedy plant growth.

Native. Inherent to an area.

Nematode. An unsegmented threadlike worm in soil; it can be beneficial or not.

Node. A joint on a stem where a leaf or branch is growing or attached.

Open pollinated. Uncontrolled pollination, where plants can interbreed.

Perennial. A plant that can survive more than two years.

pH. A logarithmic measurement of acidity and alkalinity.

Photosynthesis. A chemical process that converts light energy to food from carbon dioxide and oxygen.

Rhizome. A fleshy underground stem with buds.

Root flare. The transition zone between trunk and roots; typically the trunk widens slightly at this point.

Rosette. A crown of leaves close to the ground.

Runner. A trailing shoot that can root from the tip and nodes.

Samara. A dry fruit with a wing that contains a seed, typically from a maple or an ash.

Seed. A ripened fertilized egg containing an embryo.

Shrub. A woody plant that produces branches or shoots from the base.

Side-dressing. Applying fertilizer or compost along the side of a growing plant.

Species. An identifiable group of similar plants that produce similar offspring with minor differences.

Sport. A plant or branch showing marked difference from the normal plant.

Sterile. Not able to produce seed.

Stolon. A horizontal stem that can root and produce a new plant.

Succulent. Fleshy tissue that is soft in texture.

Sucker. A rapid-growing, upright secondary shoot growing from a stem or root.

Tilth. A description of the ability of soil to hold and release water and oxygen.

Tree. Usually a one-stemmed woody plant growing at least 12 to 15 feet tall.

Transpiration. The loss of water vapor from plants, usually through their leaf pores.

Twig. A shoot of a woody plant representing this season's growth.

Variety. An identifiable clone or subdivision of a species of plant.

Vein. Vascular rib on a leaf.

Weed. Any plant you don't want.

Index

watering, 137–38

water gardens, 139

cool-season plants, 41–42, 145

Cooperative Extension
service, 9–10, 148–49,
159, 165–66
master gardener program,
166

crape myrtle, 85

Creasy, Rosalind, 149

creeks and streams, 34

daffodils, 108–11

dahlias (winter storage), 135

Daniels, Lee, 4, 5, 6, 17

Darke, Rick, 35, 121, 123–24,
175

deciduous plants, 38

deer, 64, 94, 95, 96, 110, 120,
130, 131, 132, 144, 154–55

design
daffodil drifts, 109
deciduous and evergreen
proportions, 41
ground covers, 13
kinds of gardens, 43–46
low-maintenance gardens,
46–50
with perennials, 116–17

Dillion, Debbie, 8

dogwood, native, 76–77

Donna's best advice, 11, 13,
58, 62, 109, 139

drainage, 26, 92

drought dormancy, 29–30, 67

dry creeks, 44

Eck, Joe, and Wayne
Winterrowd, 149

evergreen plants, 39

fertilizers, 12–19

frost covers, 28, 31

frost on slopes, 33

garden books, 29, 172–74

garden Web sites, 175

Gibb, Kathy, 93, 102, 136

Goatley, Mike, 124, 125

grasses, lawn, 118, 124–25
alternatives to, 125–26

grasses, ornamental, 118–24
fertilizing, 119
for shade, 121–22
for sun, 122–23
maintenance, 119–20
miscanthus warning,
123–24
planting, 119

green roofs, 46

Green Springs Garden Park, 95

grit, 116

ground covers, 13, 47–48, 61,
62–63, 78, 84
for dry shade, 36

growing degree days, 163–64

hail, 28